RENOIR

DISCOVERING ART

The Life, Times and Work of the World's Greatest Artists

RENOIR

K. E. SULLIVAN

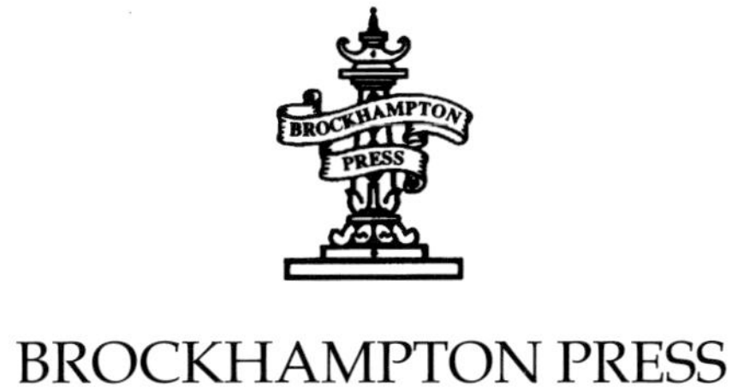

BROCKHAMPTON PRESS

For Luke

First published in Great Britain by Brockhampton Press,
a member of the Hodder Headline Group,
20 Bloomsbury Street, London WC1B 3QA

ISBN 1 86019 110 X

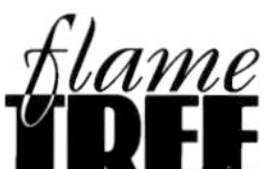

Produced by Flame Tree Publishing,
The Long House, Antrobus Road, Chiswick, London W4 5HY
for Brockhampton Press
A Wells/McCreeth/Sullivan Production

Pictures printed courtesy of the Visual Arts Library, London,
and Edimedia, Paris.

Printed and bound by Oriental Press, Dubai

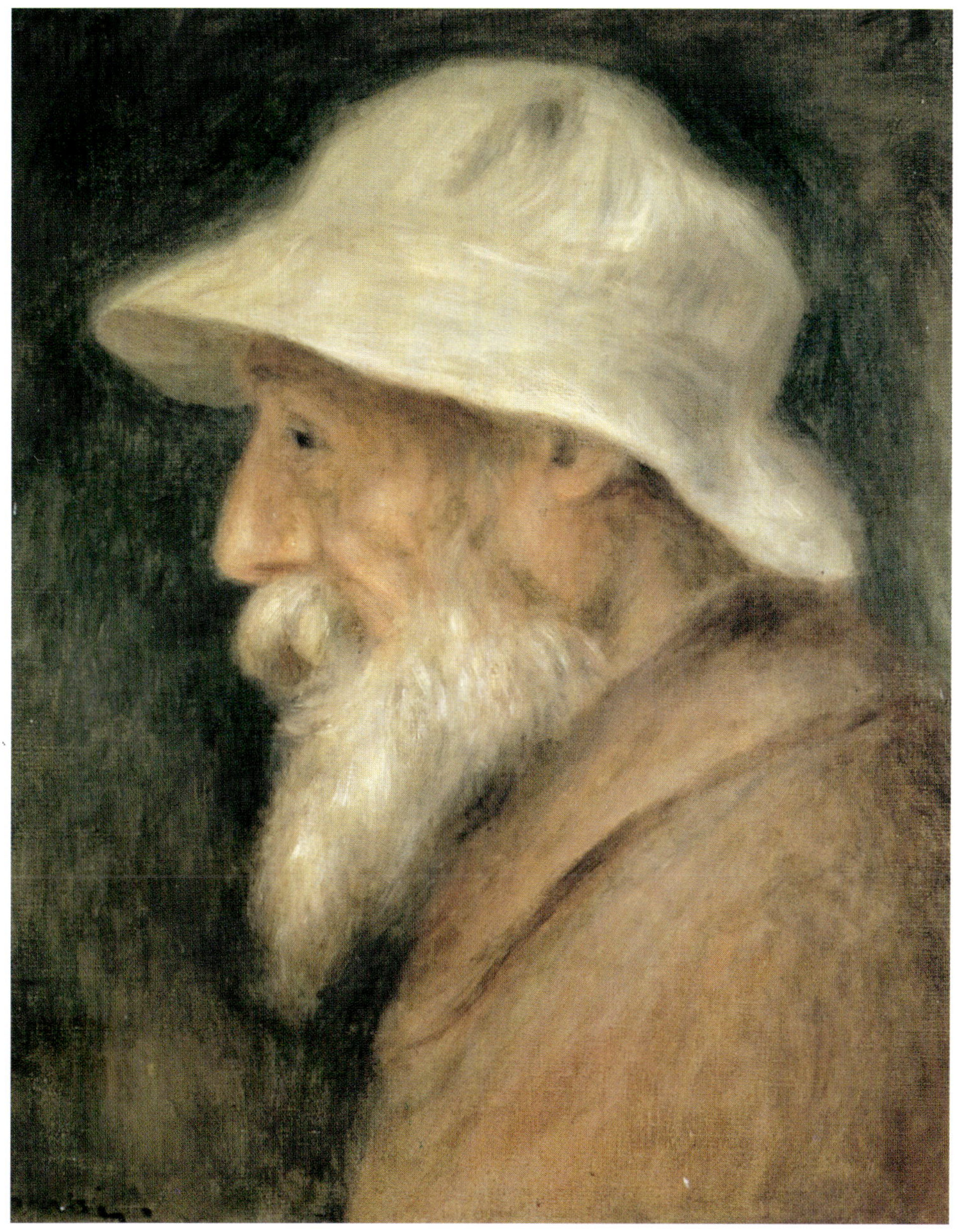

CONTENTS

Self-portrait, 1910 (Private collection).

CHRONOLOGY

Mlle Legrand, 1875 (Philadelphia Museum of Art). Renoir's portraits of children are exquisitely rendered; he applied Impressionist techniques to landscapes and portraits alike.

1841	Pierre-Auguste Renoir born in Limoges, central France.
1844	The Renoir family moves to Paris.
1854	Begins work as an apprentice decorative painter on porcelain.
1861	Begins to study in the studio of Charles Gleyre, where he meets Monet, Bazille and Sisley.
1862	Enters the Ecole des Beaux Arts.
1864	Exhibits first paintings at the Paris Salon.
1867	Moves into a flat at 20 rue Visconti with Bazille, and, soon after, Monet.
1880	Renoir begins to spend time with his companion, Aline Charigot, a seamstress who poses for him.
1881	Durand-Ruel, a wealthy art dealer, begins to buy Renoir's paintings with some regularity, reducing the financial pressures that had previously plagued the artist.
1881	Visits Italy and suffers a creative crisis.
1882	Works with Cézanne in the South of France, the first of many such excursions.
1882	Rents an apartment in Algeria, where he has travelled for health reasons.
1884–7	Renoir's Dry Period, *periode aigre*, in which he seeks to reintroduce form and line into his work.
1885	Pierre Renoir is born to Renoir and Aline Charigot.
1886	Durand-Ruel organizes Renoir's first New York exhibition at his galleries there.
1890	Marries Aline Charigot.
1890s	The early years are marked by trips to Spain; later, he pays visits to Beyreuth, Dresden and eventually Holland.
1893	Meets Jeanne Baudot and she becomes his pupil.
1894	Jean Renoir is born.
1899	Renoir is increasingly affected by crippling arthritis and begins to spend long winters on the Mediterranean coast.
1901	Claude Renoir is born.
1903	Various forgeries and fakes of Renoir's work are discovered.
1904	Renoir's first retrospective at Salon d'Automne confirms his reputation as one of France's foremost painters.
1905	Exhibits at Salon d'Automne, where he is honorary president.
1907	Purchases Les Collettes at Cagnes, in the South of France; Aline and Renoir build a large home here.
1914	Pierre and Jean are wounded in the First World War; Aline Renoir is deeply affected and becomes ill.
1915	Aline Renoir dies.
1919	Renoir is made a Commandeur de la Légion d'Honneur.
1919	Renoir dies at his home in Cagnes.

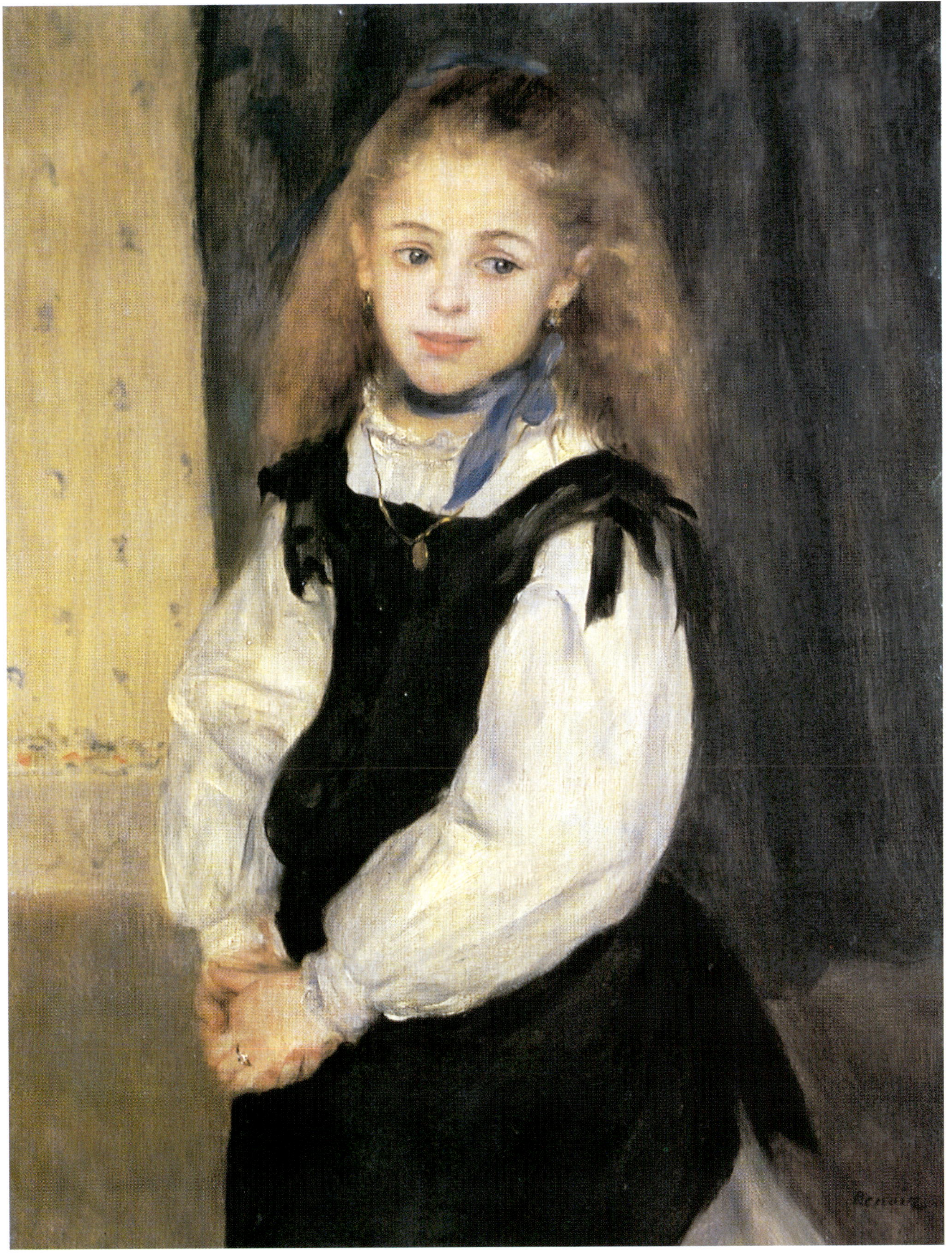
Renoir

CHAPTER 1

Conviction

'What goes on inside my head doesn't interest me. I want to touch ... or at least to see!'

Renoir

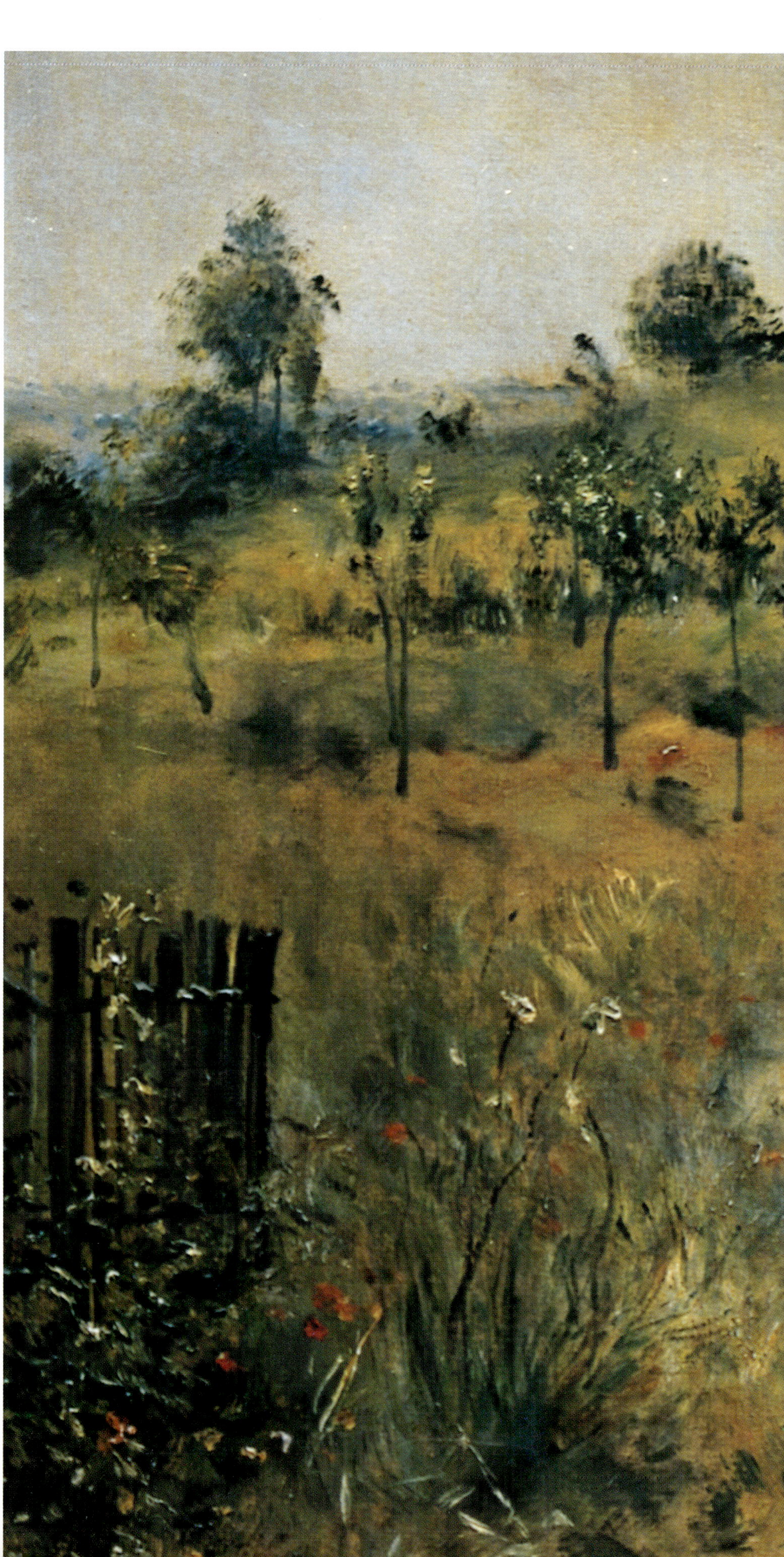

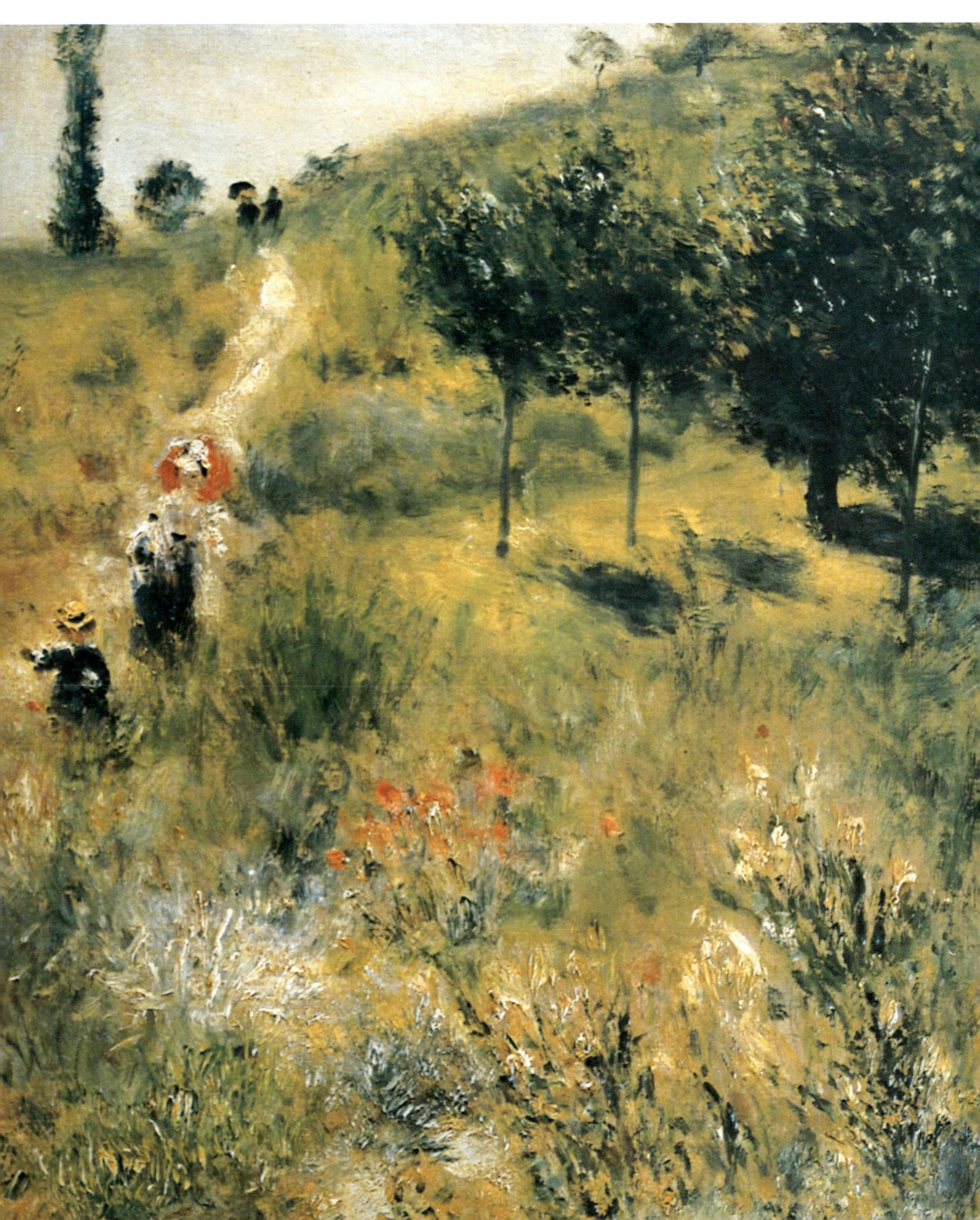

Overleaf:
The Path Among the Grass, *c.* 1875
(Musée d'Orsay, Paris). Painted while the Impressionists were suffering a barrage of critical hostility, this lovely work betrays no ill-feelings or frustration that must have been experienced by Renoir. Instead, it is a celebration of light and atmosphere in nature, illustrating everything that made the Impressionist technique so popular in years to come.

The youngest of the Impressionists, Pierre-Auguste Renoir was born on 25 February 1841, in the French town of Limoges. His family moved to Paris when Renoir was only four, and he always considered himself a Parisian, despite the fact that his roots lay further west. He was sixth in a line of seven children, and born to a tailor, Leonard Renoir, who struggled in a climate of ever-changing technological advances to keep his young family in food and lodgings. Two of Renoir's siblings had died in infancy, and the others grew up in a slum. In Paris, their home was a small apartment, curiously situated between the Louvre and the famous Tuileries gardens, which allowed the young Renoir access both to the great paintings which would later inspire him, and the splendid gardens of King Louis-Philippe, which kindled in him the great love of gardens that was shared by many of his Impressionist colleagues.

Early in life, Renoir exhibited a talent for music, which was encouraged by Charles Gounod (then undiscovered), and he was offered a place in the choir of the church of Saint-Eustache. Renoir's parents, however, recognized his superior gift for art and he was apprenticed instead to a porcelain painter, M. Levery of Levy frères et Compagnie. Porcelain painting required a keen eye and a delicate brushstroke, both of which were fostered in Renoir and would later become emblematic of his style. Renoir was only thirteen when he began his apprenticeship, and he remained there for four years, until the costs of handpainting porcelain became uneconomical and the industry ground to a halt.

The age of mechanization had changed forever many of the traditional trades and crafts, and Renoir was deeply and unshakeably affected by its influence. His first career in porcelain painting was brought to an untimely end, and his father's position as a bespoke tailor was continually threatened by the advance of industrial techniques. For the remainder of his life, Renoir rebelled against technology and it is likely that this first experience initiated his overwhelming interest in and love for things basic, simple and beautiful. He felt that technology had robbed society of its artisan conventions and that machine-produced goods were lacking in integrity; from that time he sought to restore the balance through his art. He wrote, 'The segments of an orange, the leaves of a tree, the petals of a flower, are never exactly identical. It would seem that every type of beauty derives its charm from its diversity.' Beauty, thought Renoir, could not be mass-produced. He sought to establish a new refinement in art; one which defended imperfection.

Renoir's early training did, however, create in him a dexterity and sureness of touch that was unparalleled among the Impressionists. Much later, when he suffered from crippling arthritis, Renoir was able to continue painting because of the very fluency of his technique.

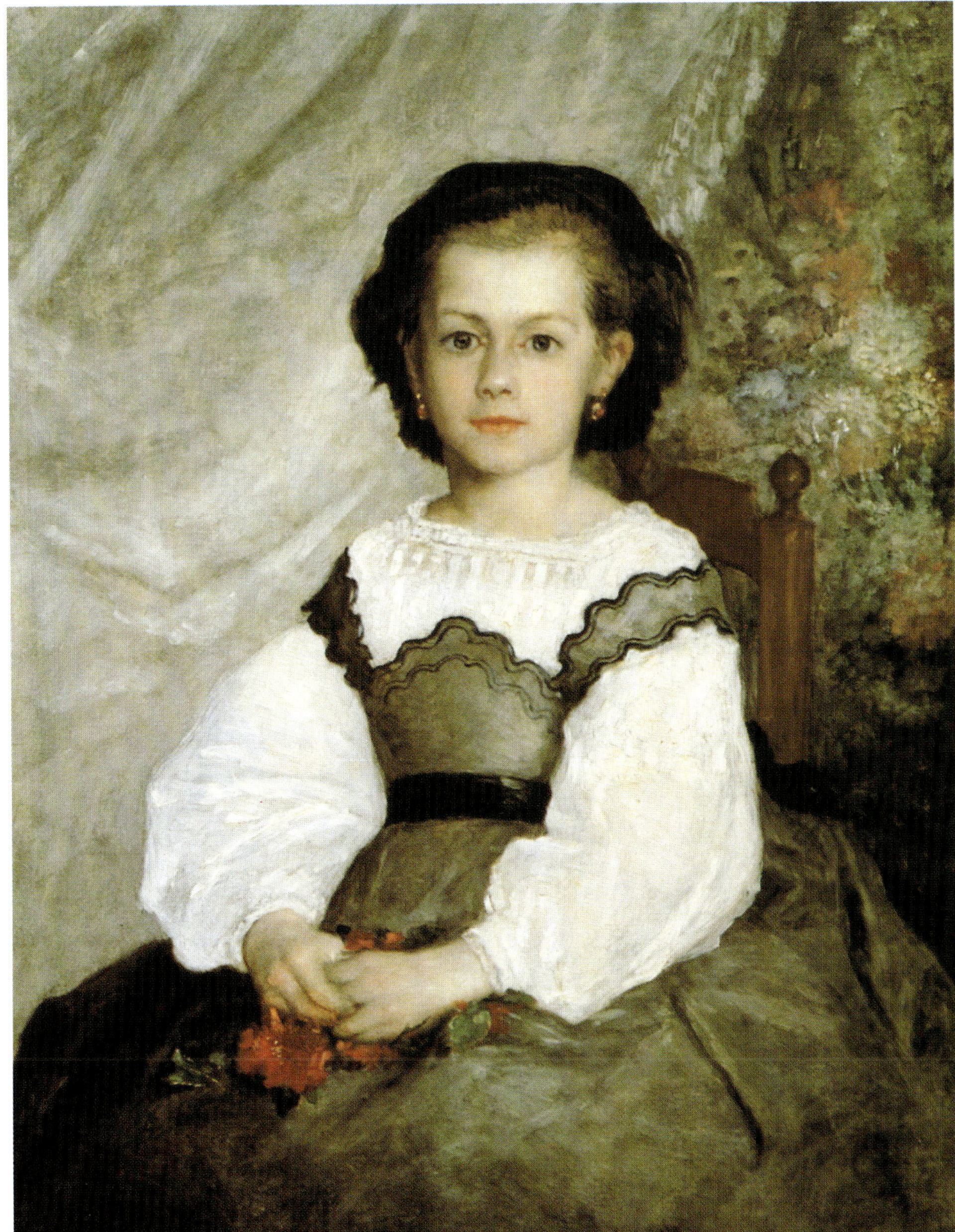

Mlle Romaine Lescaux, 1864
(Cleveland Museum of Art). Romaine Lescaux was nine when this painting was completed in 1864, the daughter of a terracotta manufacturer. It is likely that this commission came about through Renoir's porcelain work. The over-riding influence on this painting is Velázquez, but it is Renoir's own splendid talent for capturing the personality of his sitters that shines through here.

Renoir's apprenticeship left him some idle time, and he studied drawing under the sculptor Callouette. When the porcelain workshop closed, he began work with his brother, who engraved medals, where he painted coats of arms. From there he had a short career painting blinds, awnings and murals for cafés. Renoir was twenty and he'd managed to put aside some money. He longed for a career in art, but his working-class background forbade the kind of life required by a serious artist. It's fair to say that most artists in the nineteenth century were members of the middle class, relying upon external funds with which to support themselves and their art. Very few artists were able to make a decent living, or indeed live at all on what they earned from their work. Success at the Salon, the exclusive and prestigious art exhibition held annually in Paris, might guarantee some interest in an artist's work, and the possibility of some commissions, but a regular living was unlikely, and an artist's popularity could plummet overnight, if he or she were to fall out of favour with the Jury of the Salon.

Despite the daunting prospect of a penniless existence, Renoir left his regular jobs and in 1862 he was accepted at the Ecole des Beaux Arts, where he came sixty-eighth out of eighty candidates given places.

It was necessary, while studying at the Ecole, to find a suitable academic, whose techniques could be passed to the impressionable students to complement the teachings of the Ecole. Like everything else, however, this cost money, of which Renoir had little. He stumbled upon a less expensive and slightly less daunting master in the form of Charles Gleyre, a Swiss painter whose reputation also attracted three other artists who would have an incalculable impact on Renoir's life.

Claude Monet, Alfred Sisley and Frédéric Bazille were drawn to the studio of Charles Gleyre for much the same reasons as Renoir, and also because of Gleyre's relaxed principles and teaching methods. In the end, however, Monet, Bazille and Sisley lasted only a short period of time with Gleyre, Renoir being the sole member of his colleagues to remain at the studio, but it was time enough to cultivate a firm friendship. Monet would later write that Gleyre was 'of no help to his pupils ... we were well rid of it.'

Renoir was making a statement by becoming an artist. He would no longer be a tradesman, or indeed a member of the class to which he was born; he would mix in circles to which he was unaccustomed. There is some evidence that Renoir was uneasy with the society of which he had become a member. To a certain extent he shunned the trappings of any kind of prosperity, particularly that which came to him later in his professional career. As a young painter, however, he shared with his colleagues the delicious freedom that a career of painting brought to them. To be an artist in the mid-nineteenth century was a romantic and indulgent move. Bazille was supported by a tolerant and very wealthy father; Monet was dependent on his own father for a living allowance. Sisley also had parents who were keen to support their son's ambitions – and fortunately, to a certain extent, those of his friends. Renoir alone depended on the money he had earned as a tradesman and when that money ran out he often went without food.

It was, however, a life of enormous rewards; the young men spent their time and their creative energies on a job they loved and lived and breathed. The realities of the world around them were rarely allowed to encroach on the sheer pleasure of spending one's day doing what one does and loves best. Even when their reputations had become established, they did without many necessities. Renoir later wrote to Bazille, 'We don't eat every day. Yet I am happy in spite of it, because,

Lady at the Piano, *c.* 1865 (Chicago Institute of Art). In this popular painting, Renoir celebrates once again the human form. The pianist comes alive under the subtle daubs of Renoir's paintbrush. It is not surprising that his portraits would become a sought-after commodity.

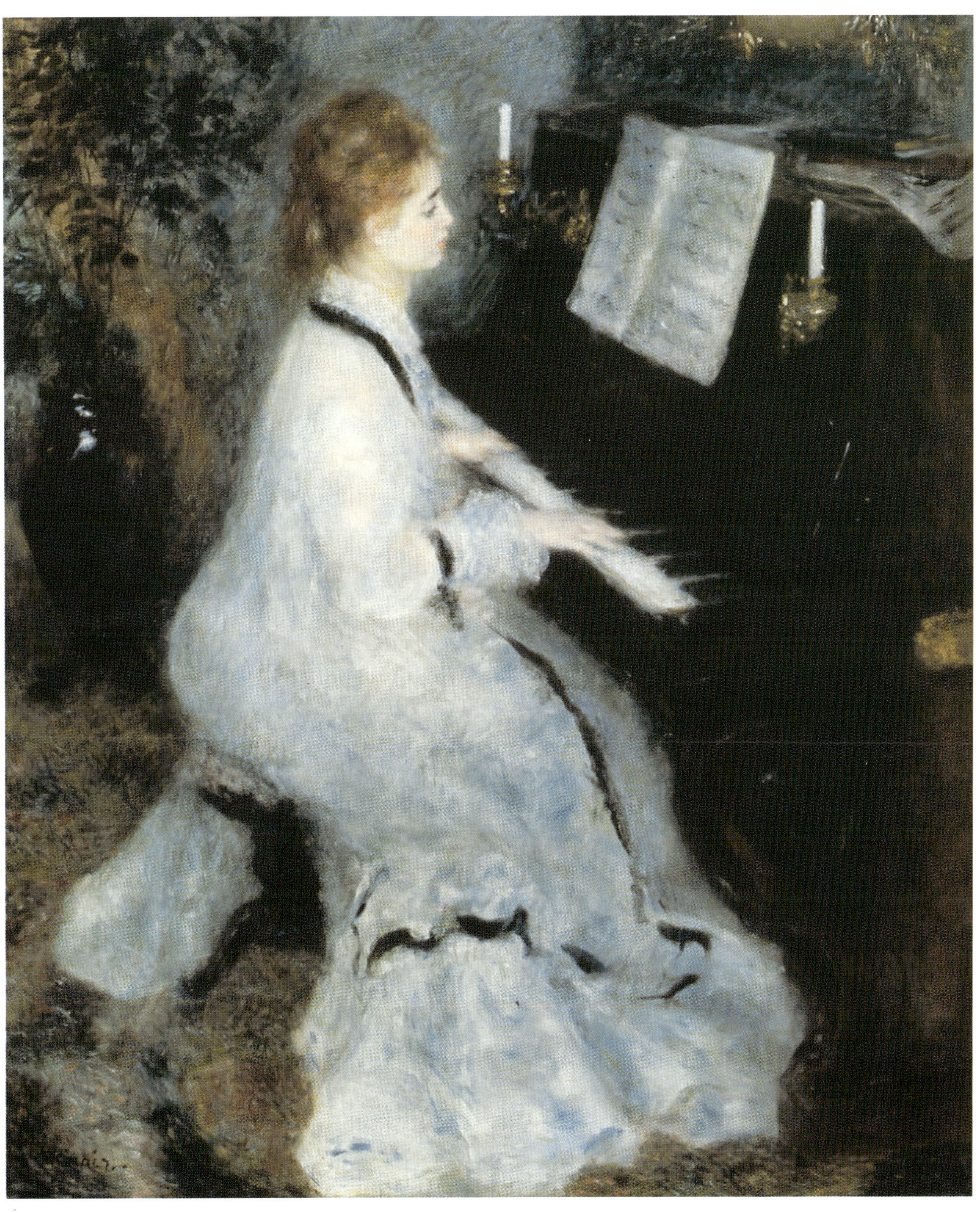

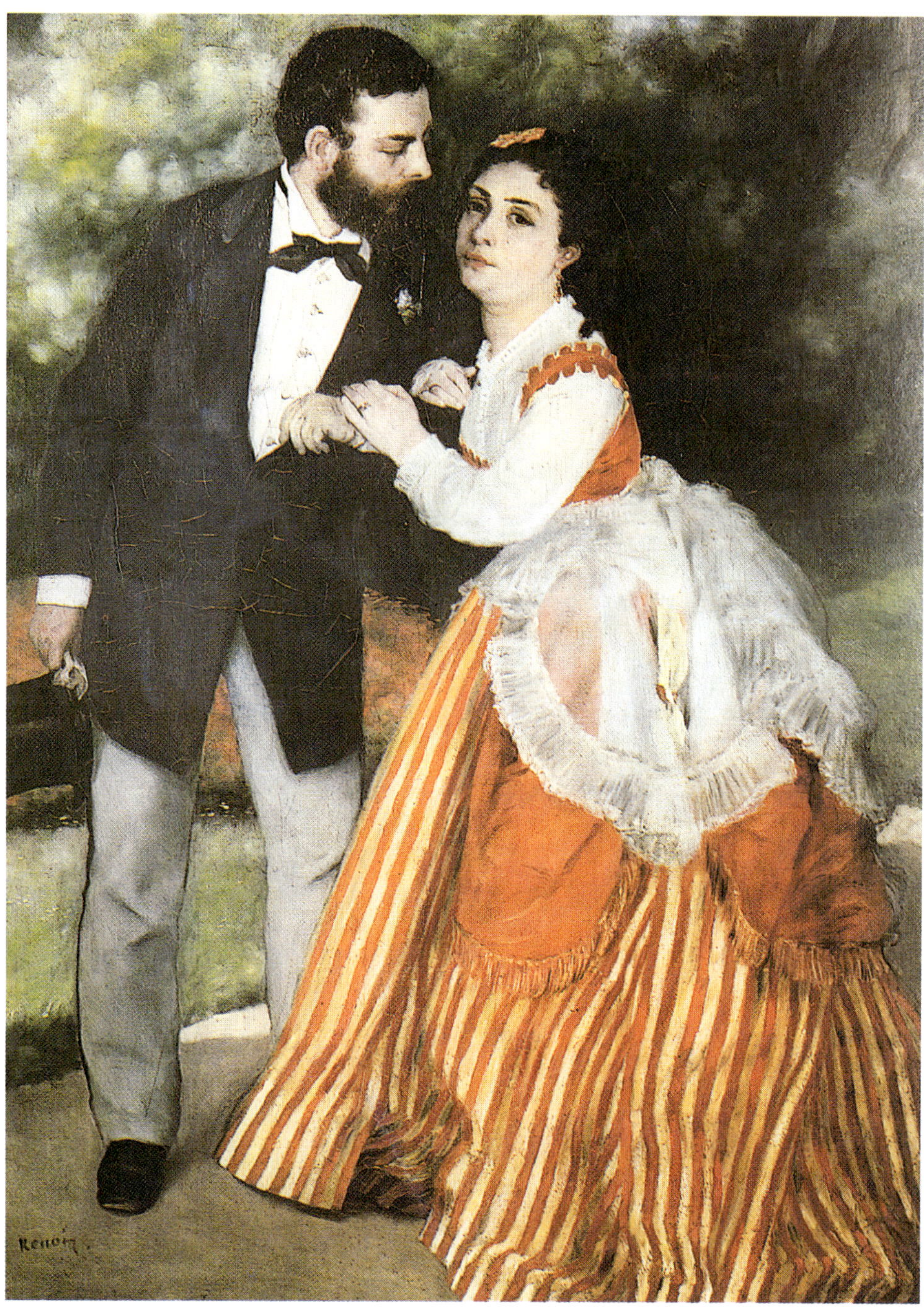

The Engaged Couple (known as **The Sisley Family) *c.* 1968** (Wallraf-Richartz Museum, Cologne). This painting, one of Renoir's most famous, takes as its subject Renoir's good friend Alfred Sisley (1839–99), and his companion Eugenie Lescouezec. It was considered by many to be Renoir's answer to Monet's *Women in the Garden*, but unlike Monet he expends little effort creating the perfect landscape or background, concentrating instead on his perfectly rendered figures.

as far as painting is concerned, Monet is good company. I do almost nothing because I have no paint.'

The four friends began painting out of doors, particularly in the forest of Fontainebleau, where they became enchanted by the effects of light and atmosphere. It was a fascination which would become the mainstay of much of the Impressionist movement, and which would captivate Monet for the rest of his life. Quite apart from the influence of his friends and their sojourns with nature in these early days, the trips to Fontainebleau had even greater significance for Renoir. It was here, in 1863, that he met the ageing painter Diaz de la Pena, whose forest scenes had won him a place with the Barbizon group of painters. Diaz, too, was interested in portraying the impression of sunlight through the trees and after his chance meeting with the artists, Renoir credited him as his first great influence. It was Diaz who suggested that Renoir lighten his palette, removing black entirely, which changed the nature of his work and the course of his art from that time onwards.

In 1864, Renoir's dedication to his art paid off. His first submission to the Salon, *Esmeralda Dancing with her Goat,* was accepted. Sadly he later destroyed this work, disliking its academicism and rigidity.

Renoir's next great influence was that of the painter Gustav Courbet, whom he met at Marlotte, near the forest of Fontainebleau. Courbet was a French painter whose later works included pleasant landscapes painted in light, engaging colours. Although his work in no way pre-empted or in any way presaged the work of the Impressionists, he had a timely effect on Renoir. This was most evident in his painting

Portrait of Alphonsine Fournaise, 1879 (Musée d'Orsay, Paris). This painting, often wrongly called *At the Grenouillère,* is an example of Renoir's superb ability to capture the enchanting *joie de vivre* of the habituées of small suburban bistros.

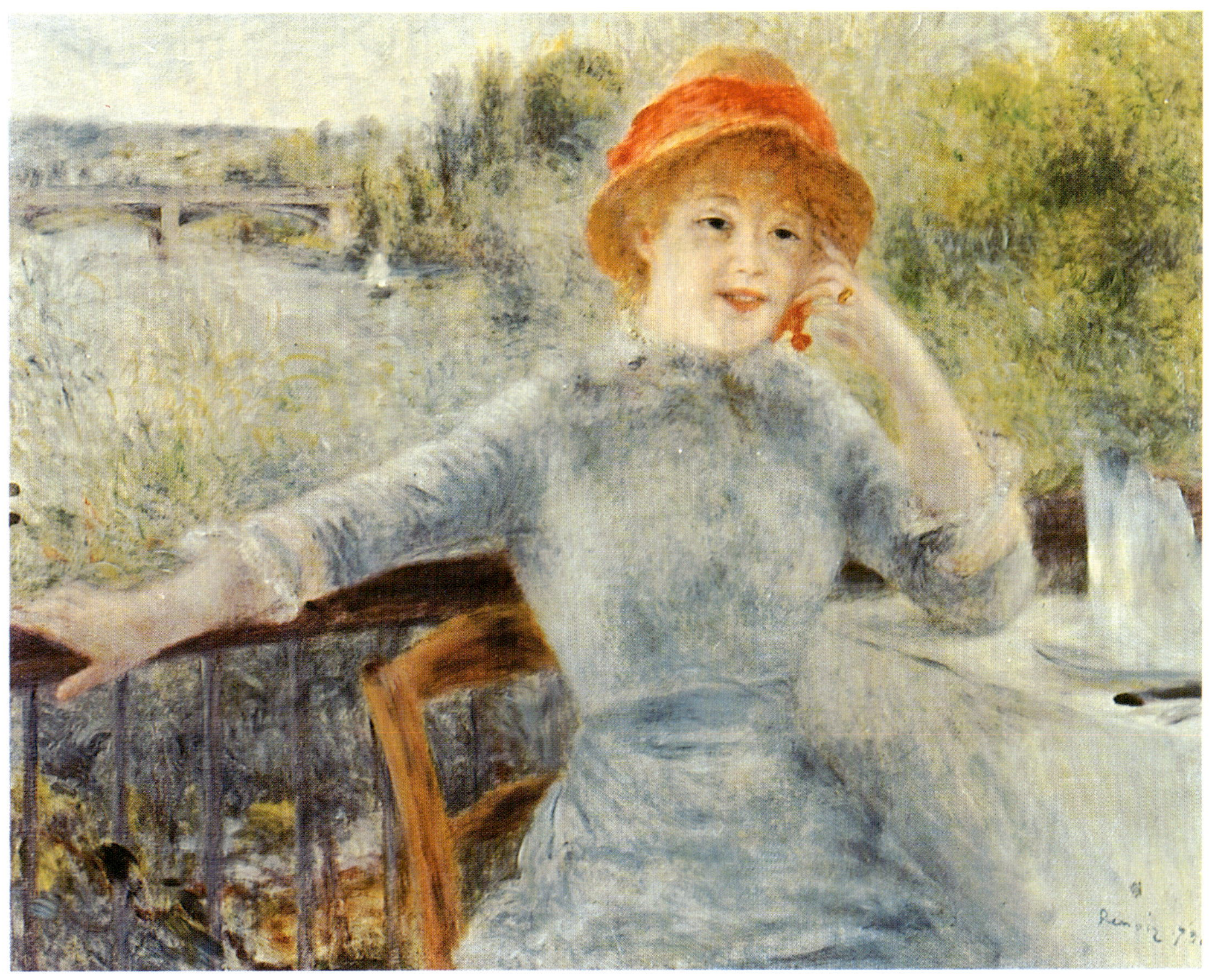

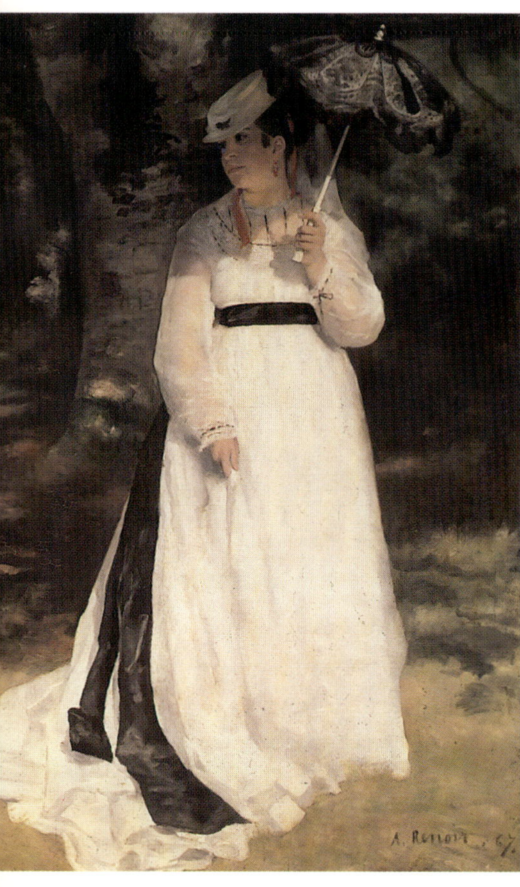

Lise with a Parasol, 1867 (Museum Folkwang, Essen, West Germany). This painting was painted in 1867 and hung at the Salon in 1868. It features Lise Tréhot, Renoir's lover and the model for much of his early work.

The Inn of Mère Anthony, rejected by the Salon in 1866. Lawrence Gowing, in 'Renoir's Sentiment and Sense', wrote:

> *Due to Courbet the Impressionist grasp of the matter of life was always much more robust than the programme, the reduction of painterly notation to its summary essence, might have suggested. Renoir's development was punctuated for years by life-sized standing figures, culminating in a sequel to Courbet's* Demoiselles aux bords de la Seine, *a nude modelled on the Medici Venus ...*

Manet was another important influence. In 1863 his famous painting *Dèjeuner sur l'Herbe* was exhibited at the Salon des Refusés, an 'alternative' exhibition created by Napoleon III, in response to the protests of artists whose work had been refused by the Salon. Manet's painting caused such a stir that it closed the exhibition, and brought him instant notoriety. He was considered the *enfant terrible* of art, but he became a guru among the young Parisian painters, who delighted in his fresh approach; Manet used paint with gay abandon and subjects that were natural, set in the present and dressed accordingly. Manet had found a champion in Baudelaire, and Renoir and his friends were new recruits to his growing ideology. It was Manet who first put into words what the Impressionists stood for, even if it was Monet's work which eventually gave it a name.

It was partly Manet's one-man show in the gallery of the famous dealer Martinet which inspired Monet, Sisley and eventually Renoir to leave the Académie Gleyre, in order to paint without supervision. The young artists were restless with the academic approach to art that was required by students of the Ecole, and indeed any of the academic masters. Gleyre was puzzled by the evident joy that Renoir, in particular, was getting from his work. In the past painting had been more of an exact science, working to known and approved theorems to produce something that was recognizable and comprehensible. Nowhere along the line had painters admitted such hedonistic delight in their art. Renoir often told the story of his exchange with Gleyre as a student: '"Doubtless you paint for your own amusement?" "Yes, I assure you that if it didn't amuse me I wouldn't do it."'

Delacroix, a French painter attributed with the evolution of the Romantic school of art, was fond of painting what was termed by many critics to be 'sensual indulgence' and this too was undertaken by Renoir, who unashamedly adopted techniques, styles and approaches from a variety of different yet equally challenging painters. Lawrence Gowing notes:

> *It was significant that all these styles were succeeding one another on Renoir's easel in the same years. None of his friends experi-*

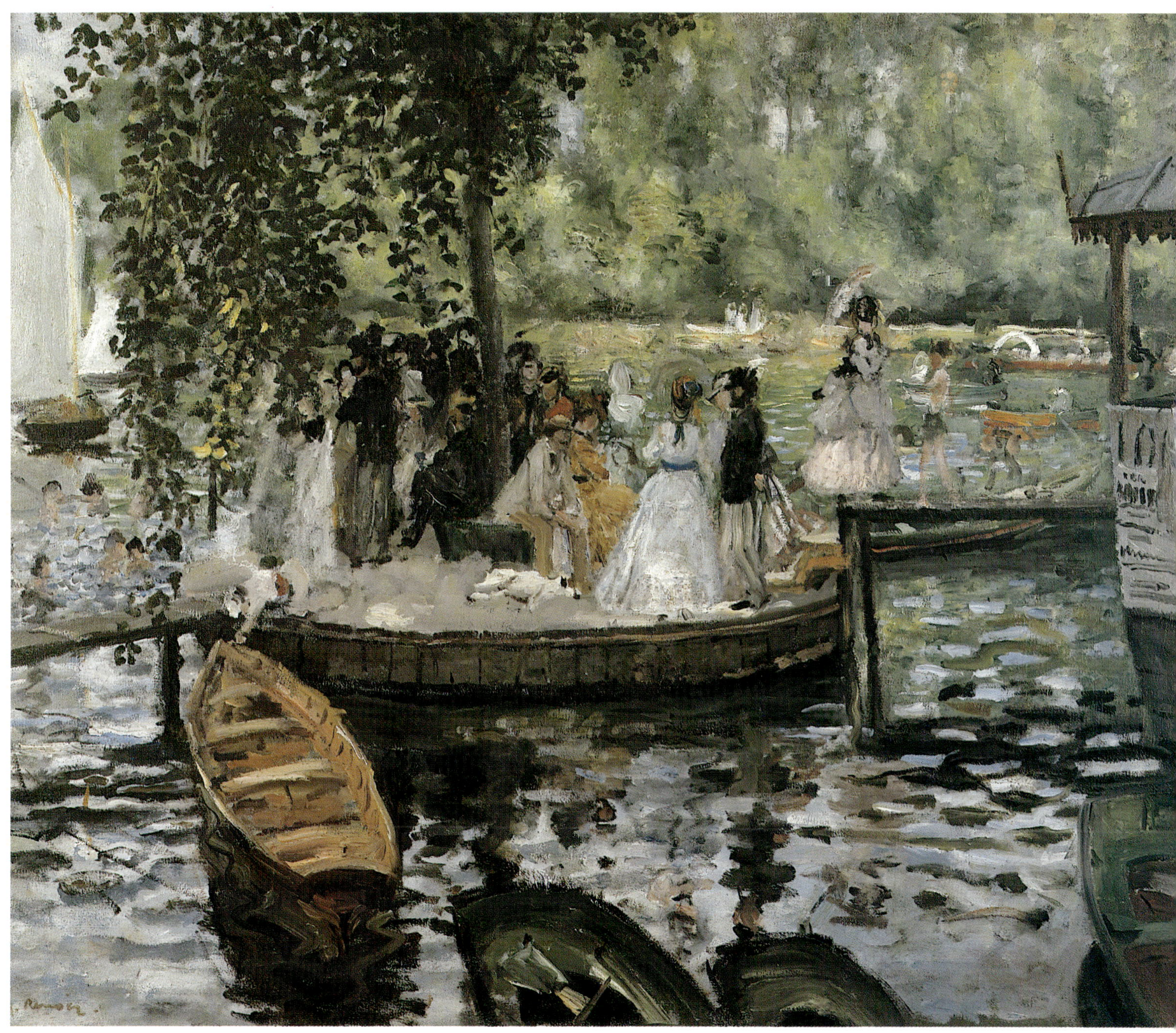

mented so widely and inconsistently. None would have cared to embark on so many different styles, or to imitate them so closely ... What gave Renoir's point of departure a commanding advantage was without doubt his capacity and determination from the first to please himself.

La Grenouillère, 1869
(Nationalmuseum, Stockholm). La Grenouillère was a popular open-air cafe and bathing establishment on the Seine. Renoir painted here with Monet and each achieved several impressions of the scene. Their work incorporated many of the elements that would become known as Impressionist, and are regarded as the first fully realized paintings of the school.

Throughout the sixties, Renoir lived with various of the friends he made at the Ecole and Gleyre's Académie. Bazille was a generous and reliable friend, sharing his studio whenever necessary, and helping to seek portrait commissions for both Renoir and Monet.

Acceptance at the Salon ensured that painters were able to get a decent sum for their work, and Renoir lived on the meagre proceeds of his commissioned work. He worked as a portrait painter for much of the sixties, many of his subjects being friends of families of his wealthier colleagues, or the result of subtle gestures from the friends of his own family. Unlike many of the more sober commissioned portraits undertaken many of his contemporaries, Renoir's portraits are bursting with the life that would one day trademark his work. In the 1865 Salon exhibition was a portrait of the father of his friend Sisley. He also painted Bazille, and Renoir's friend Jules Le Coeur had a wealthy family who would commission work from the young artist from time to time.

It's likely that Renoir originally accepted these commissions in order to scrape a living, but the exuberance with which they are rendered reveals the enjoyment he clearly gained from painting them. For Renoir loved to paint and any opportunity which allowed it, which generated enough money to purchase more canvas, more paint, more free time, was sheer pleasure.

Renoir painted, sought new commissions, visited friends across the country, took any excuse for a change of scene. His wanderlust was legendary. He stayed with Sisley in Le Havre, and they developed a strong friendship. Sisley was a charming man, more interested in landscapes than his friend Renoir, whose interest in the human form was evolving even then, and Sisley's great fondness for women was famed. Renoir later told his son Jean that Sisley 'could never resist a petticoat. We would be walking along the street, talking about the weather or something equally trivial and suddenly Sisley would disappear. Then I would discover him at his old game of flirting.'

Renoir also stayed with his friend, the painter Jules Le Coeur, in Marlotte, where he met Lise Tréhot, the sister of Le Coeur's mistress. Lise became his own mistress, and the model for a number of his paintings, sharing his life for five years between 1866 and 1871, and appearing again and again in his work. Her image has become identified with this period of his life; she posed for various paintings such as *The Bather with Griffon*, *Diana (The Huntress)*, and *Odalisque*. *Lise with a Parasol* was painted in 1867, and hung at the Salon in 1868. The reviews were mixed, but a number of critics accused him of copying Manet, and still others Whistler and Courbet. Renoir had not yet found his own artistic identity – his subject matters were very much decided by whatever else was in favour with the Jury at the Salon, and his style was often dependent upon the company he was keeping.

Renoir lived with Bazille in a studio in Paris, where they were soon joined by Monet, who was temporarily out of favour with his family, and moved again to a studio and heated room in the Batignolles district of Paris, near the Café Guérbois, which was the current meeting place of the group of artists led by Manet. Bazille was pleased to

Nude in the Sunlight, 1876 (Musée d'Orsay, Paris). Renoir showed this painting at the second Impressionist exhibition in 1876. Several sympathetic critics admired the delicate rendering of the flesh tones; most despised Renoir's vision, one likening his use of colour on the flesh to 'a mass of decomposing flesh with the green and purplish blotches that indicate a state of complete putrefaction ...'

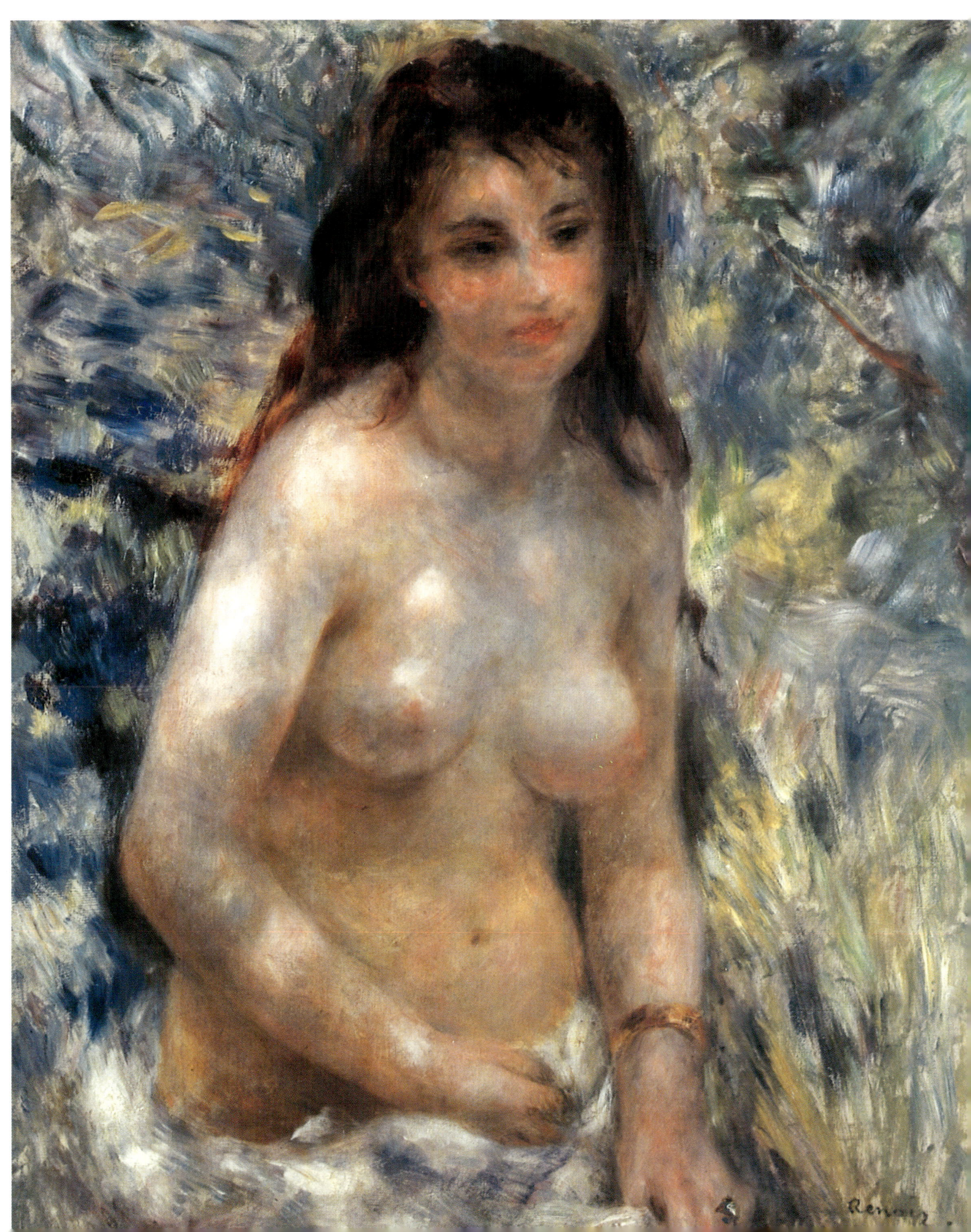

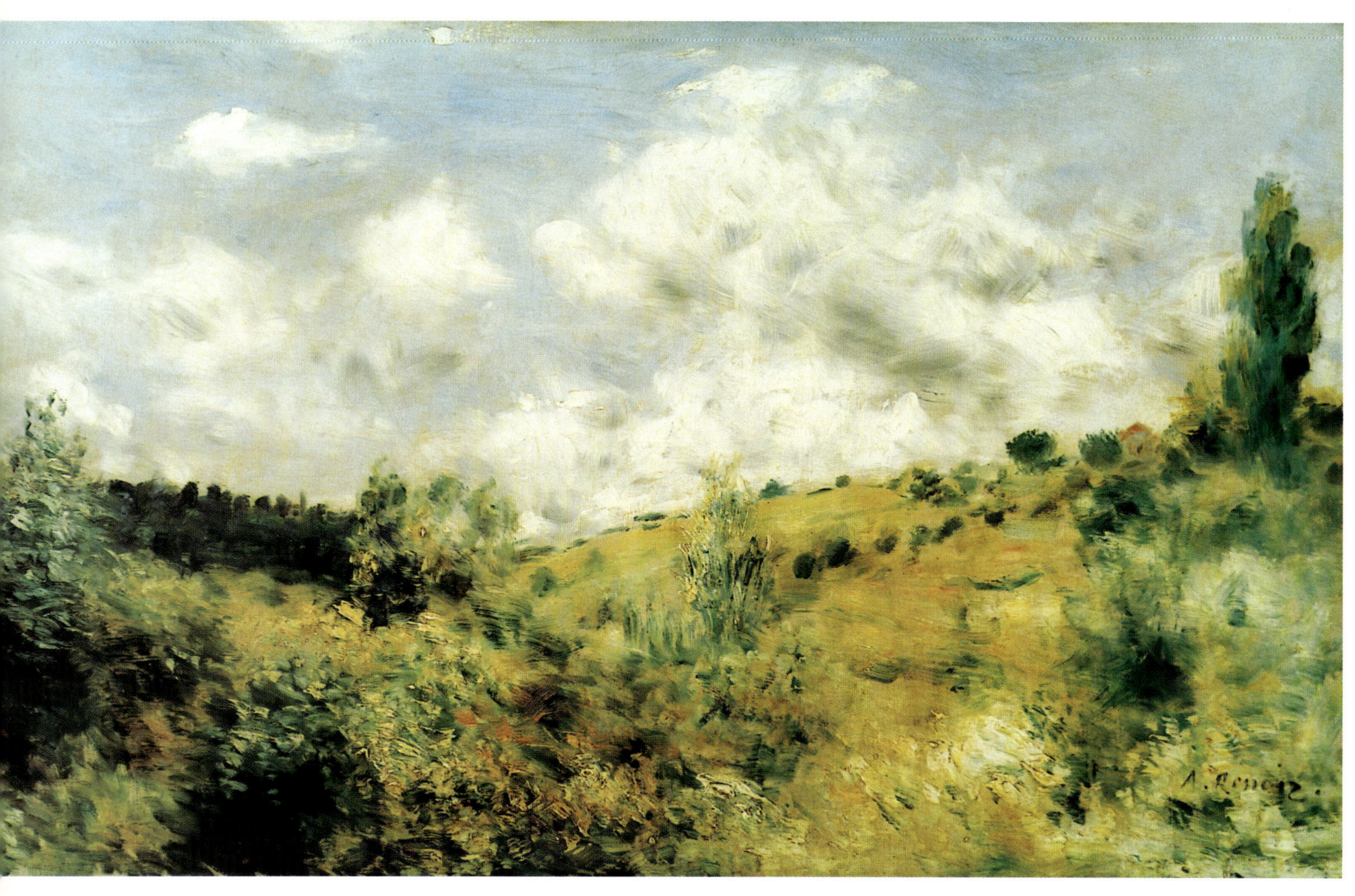

The Gust of Wind, ***c.*** **1873** (Fitzwilliam Museum, Cambridge). An exceptionally evocative impression of a summer's day, this work was painted just before the first Impressionist exhibition when Renoir's Impressionist technique was at its height.

Opposite:
Little Blue Nude, 1878 (Private collection). Renoir's fascination with the female form began in the early years of his art. Here he applies Impressionist techniques to his model, only just beginning to implement the use of contours which would later distinguish his work.

take the needy artists under his wing. He wrote to his sister, 'Monet has fallen upon me from the skies. Counting Renoir, that makes two hard-working painters I'm housing. I'm delighted.'

In 1969, Renoir went to live with his parents for a short time at Voisins-Louveciennes, from where he travelled to meet Monet at his home near Bougival. They painted here together at La Grenouillère and it was throughout this period that the first whispers of Impressionism made themselves heard.

La Grenouillère, on the River Seine, near Paris, was a favourite outdoor café, bathing spot and meeting place, frequented by fun-seeking sunbathers. It was within commuting distance of Paris, and it was a popular haunt for city-dwellers and country folk alike. Monet and Renoir often sat side by side, their easels nearly touching, painting the same scenes over and over again. These are the paintings that set the standards for everything that Impressionism would become – animated, open-air scenes of everyday life, rippling with energy, colour and laughter. The artists painted on the spot, capturing the effect of the sunlight on water, dappling in figures as merrily as touches of light. They sought to seize a moment, to recreate it in a

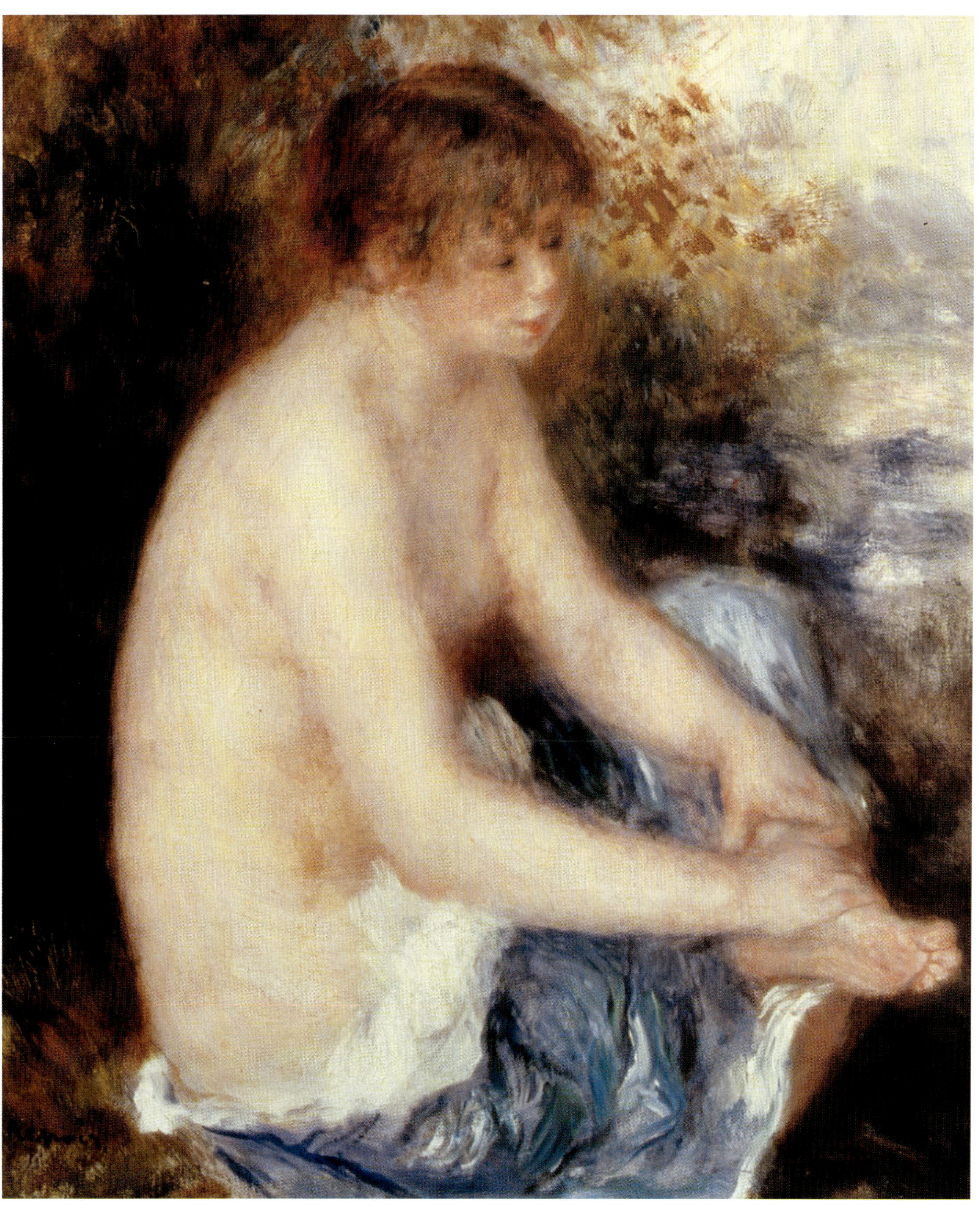

painting that was as vibrant as the scene itself. Gone were the heavy contours and shadows of previous schools of art.

These pre-Impressionist paintings had the spontaneity of a photograph, but the visionary impact of something much more subtle. The artists didn't seek realism, recreating instead the effect of a brief period of time with daubs of colour and light that represent clearly the conditions of that moment. Patches of diverse colour intimated the impression of the scene. Accents of colour replaced drawing, and touches of paint took the place of any kind of formal structure. Critics of the day considered these paintings grossly unfinished.

Renoir was the most energetic of his contemporaries and had learned from Boudin how to see and paint a landscape under natural lighting conditions. He despised the cold light of the studio and cheerfully he would go on to apply the Impressionist techniques to all his works – portraits, nudes and landscapes alike. He was responsible, encouraged by Diaz de le Pena, for the introduction of the 'Rainbow Palette', which restricted the use of colour to pure tones of maximum intensity, with the elimination of black.

Monet wrote to Bazille in Autumn of 1869, outlining his plans for the next Salon exhibition: 'I do have a dream, a painting of the bathing place at La Grenouillère. I have made a few poor sketches, but it is no more than a dream. Renoir, who has just spent two months here, also wants to paint the same picture.' Ironically it was those very sketches which, unchanged, represent some of the most typical work of the Impressionists.

Many of these early works had the feel of a sketch; indeed, the artists themselves considered them to be the forerunners to greater works which they would later complete. They painted quickly, before the scene altered, before the light changed. Some of their paintings were reworked in the studio, but in general they remained as fresh and vivid as the moment they were painted. Dozens of paintings were created in these heady days; as long as there was money for a bit of paint, and a day free of rain, the artists were happy to sit and work, sharing food if there was any, banter alone, if there was not.

Monet would become obsessed with painting out of doors, with capturing every aspect of light and atmosphere. While Renoir continued to paint landscapes, he found more pleasure in people and much of his work was characterized by the human form. Renoir's style differed from Monet's and each of their paintings, even those worked at the same moment, can be immediately distinguished. Renoir was fascinated by the techniques and inspiration of both his contemporaries and past masters. No other artist so openly adopted the styles of others, but these amalgamations of style and method became so quintessentially Renoir that all was forgiven. He loved to paint; he experimented, emulated, took risks. It was a sensual experience; small

Woman Reading, 1874 (Musée d'Orsay, Paris). 1874 was a prolific years for Renoir. He painted many works portraying women in repose, and this one in particular reflects his casual and supremely peaceful interpretation of a familiar scene.

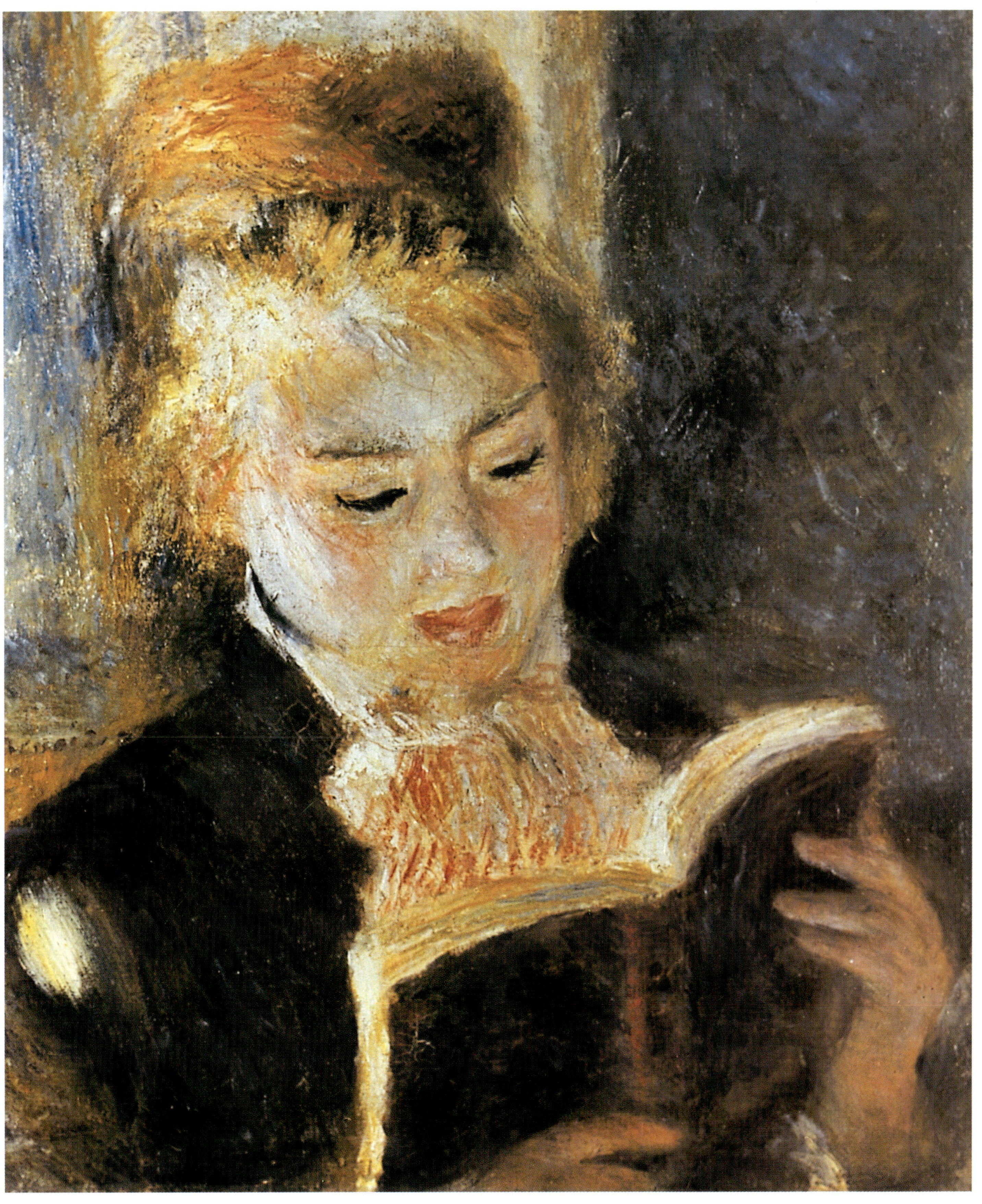

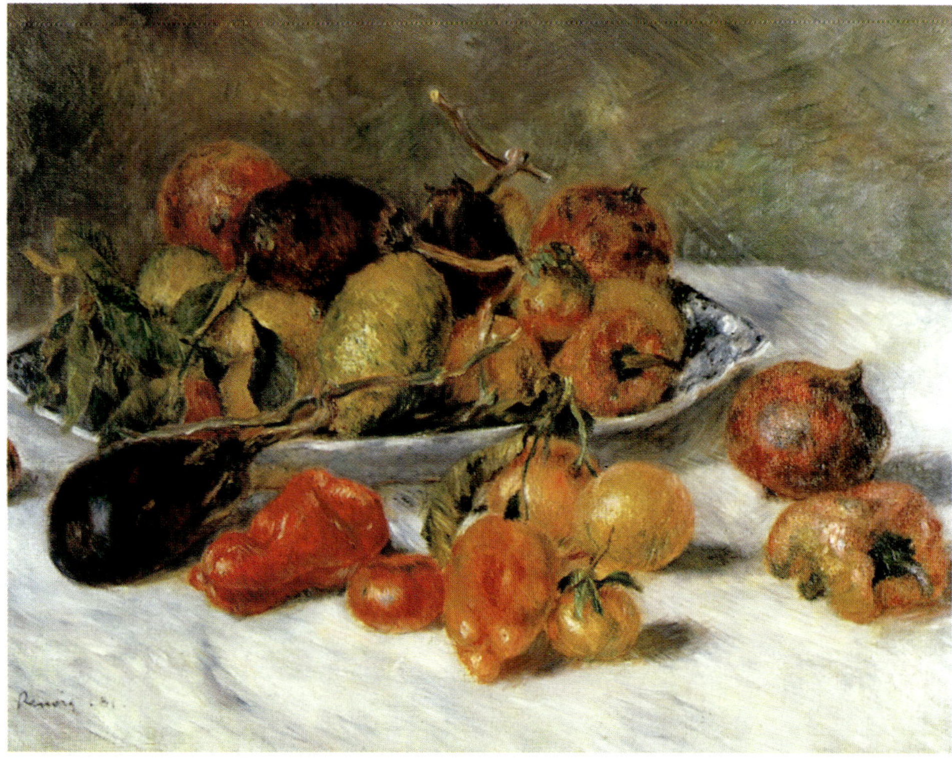

Fruits from the Midi, 1881 (Chicago Institute of Art). Painted in the year which saw the beginning of Renoir's *periode aigre* this exquisite still-life seeks a symmetry of form that was missing from his earlier, more spirited work. The influence of Cézanne is evident.

erotic brushstrokes, tempered by long caressing sweeps of paint. He said, 'It's with my brush that I make love. My pictures should make me want to stroll in it, if it is a landscape, or to stroke a breast if it is a figure.' He felt that a painting should give the viewer as much pleasure as he found in its conception. Jules Le Coeur's sister noted that he was like a 'body without spirit when he has nothing underway'. Renoir himself said later, to Albert André, one of his interviewers:

> *Painting is done to decorate walls. So it should be as rich as possible. For me a picture – for we are forced to paint easel pictures – should be something likeable, joyous and pretty – yes, pretty. There are enough ugly things in life for us not to add to them. I well realize that it is difficult for painting to be accepted as really great painting whilst remaining joyous.*

The seventies were tough years financially, but there was a spirit of optimism nurtured by the group of friends who would one day become some of the most famous artists in history, creating a school of painting which would charm hundreds of people down the centuries, and change forever the definition of art. These painters expressed a *joie de vivre* that was fast becoming an important aspect of their generation. They painted life as they saw it around them: the glorious days of entertainment and the babble of café society at its height. Impressionism evokes colour and sunlight, good food and clever, assertive minds. Prewar France was a mecca for young and philosophical men and women, and their burgeoning ideas are echoed in the paintings that depict them.

Renoir in particular managed to catch the glittering activity of both people and place, the hazy, atmospheric glow of colour, the flirtatious effect of light on the water, the leaves, the air, and the movement and sound vibrating from the smiling young men and women who chat and eat and dance and most importantly enjoy.

These vigorous and exciting days were, however, about to come to an abrupt end. Renoir's *The Bather with Griffin* and *Odalisque* were accepted at the Salon, and this meant a year with a certain amount of financial security. But on 19 July 1870, the Franco-Prussian War was declared. The world of gaiety and frivolity that distinguished Renoir's and his friends; art was never the same again.

The Skiff, 1879 (National Gallery, London). This painting is pure Impressionist – broken lines of colour and a lack of contour and framework that allow the subjects to become a part of the landscape.

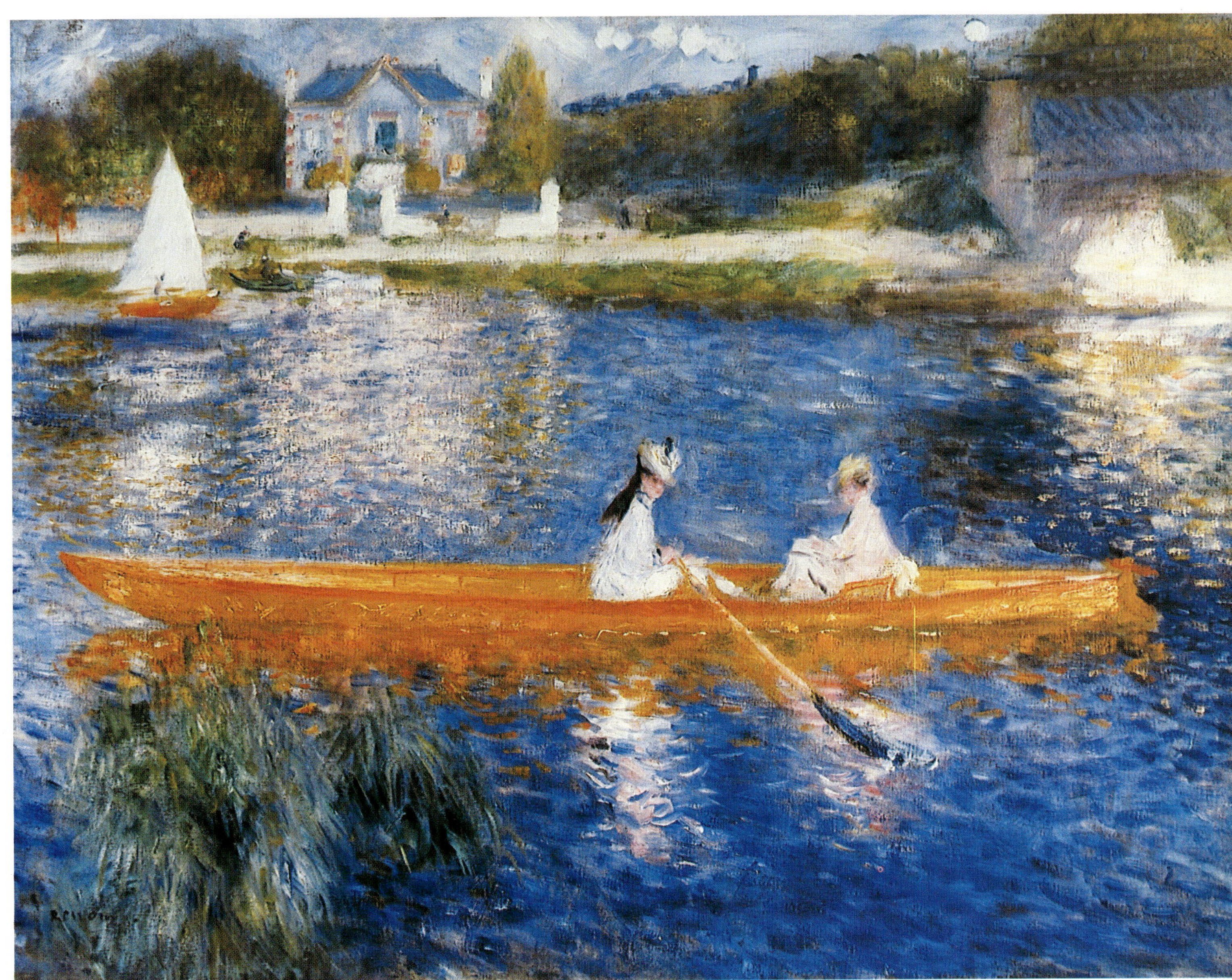

CHAPTER 2

Inspiration and Impressions

Renoir was conscripted to the Franco-Prussian War soon after its beginning. He was sent to the Pyrenees to train and care for the horses, a move which probably saved his life.

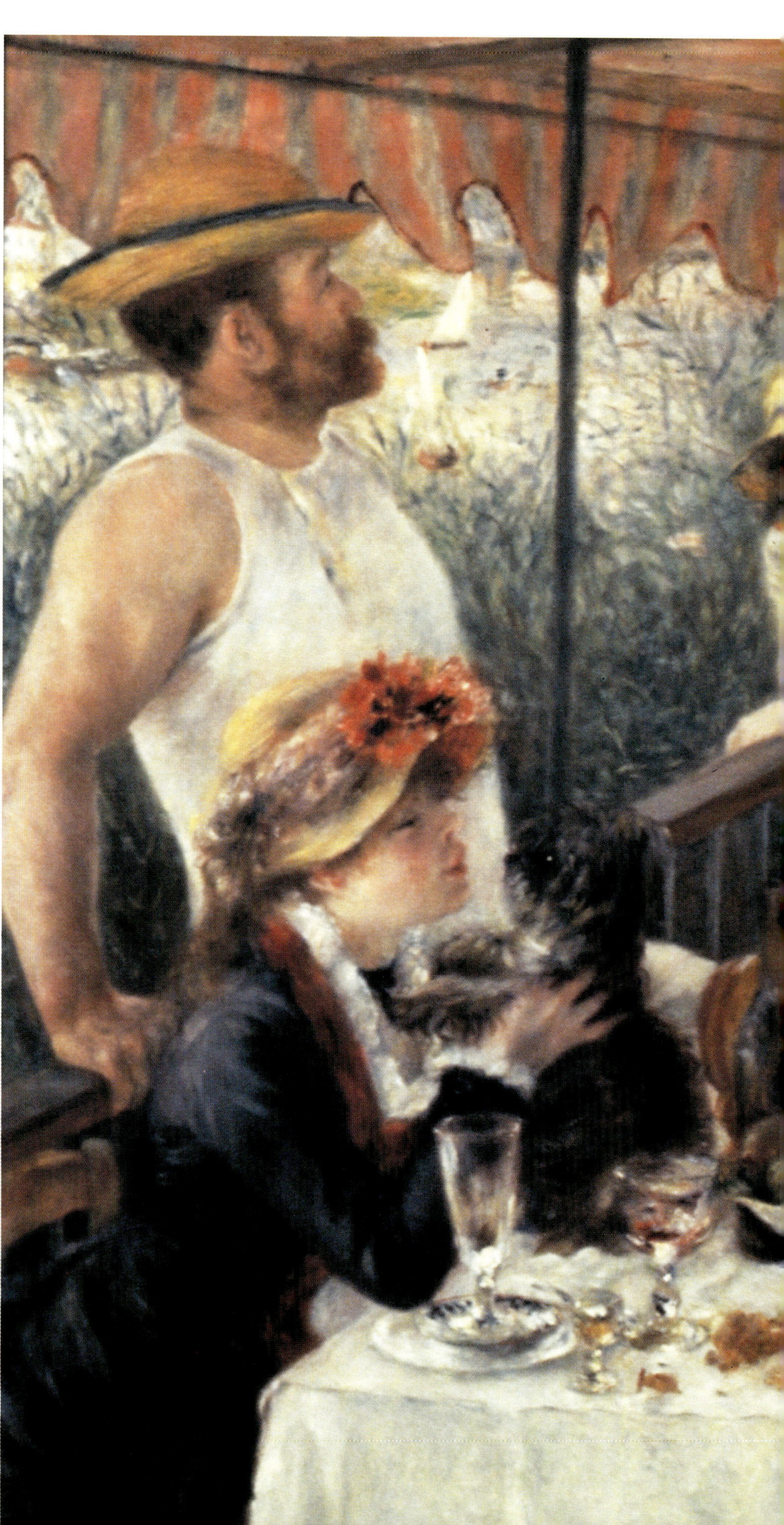

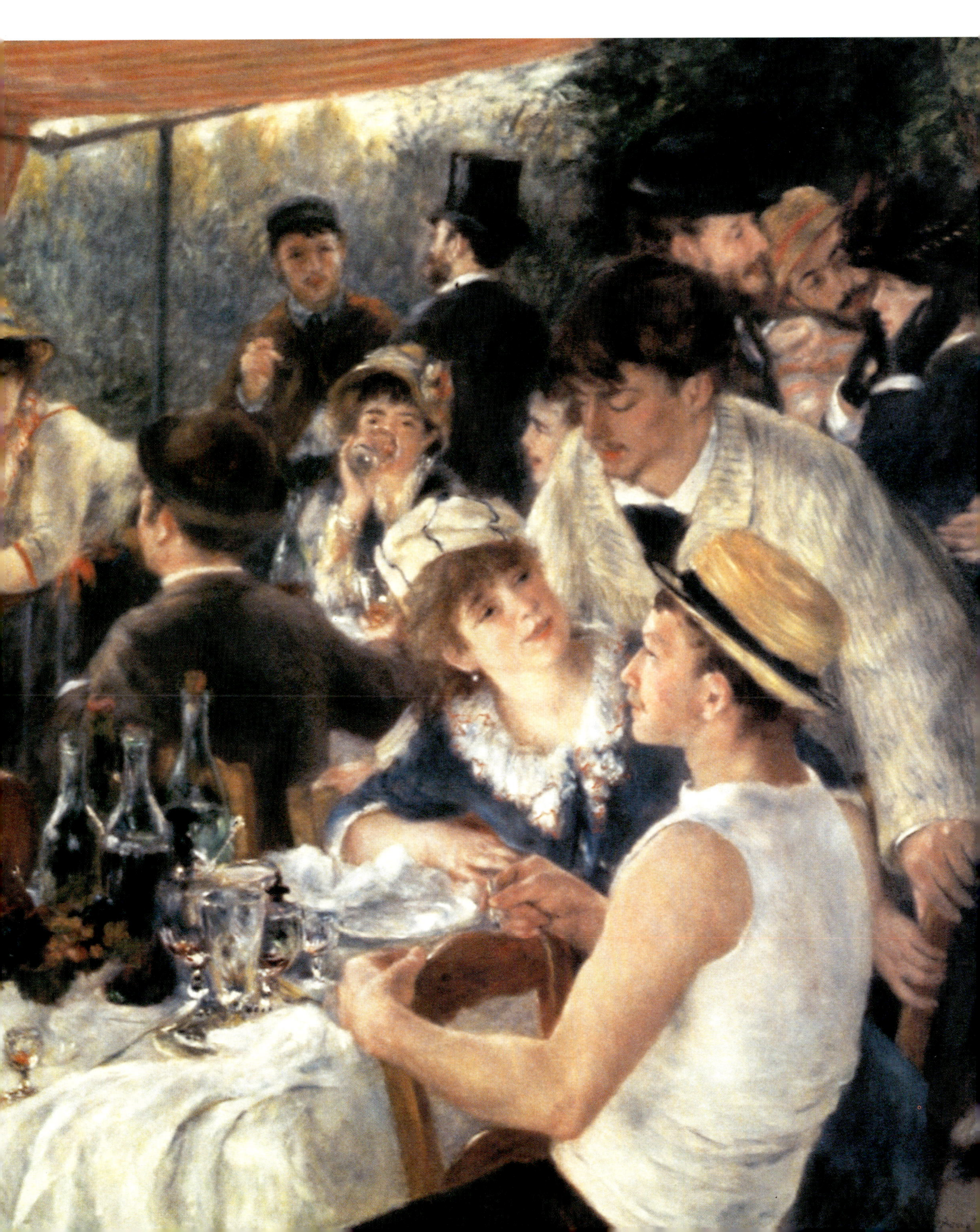

Overleaf:
Luncheon of the Boating Party, 1880-81 (Phillips Collection, Washington). This painting, which followed *Ball at the Moulin de la Galette*, reflects the changes that were beginning to occur in Renoir's work before his *periode aigre*. The painting is more structured, and its characters delineated more than in the past. His future wife, Aline Charigot, sits in the front left of the painting.

Renoir's good friend Frederic Bazille was killed in thc war and with him died all the promise of his work. Bazille had been friend, inspiration and in many ways a safety net for the young man, and Renoir was distraught by his untimely death. Bazille had always believed in Renoir; he'd once said, 'From the way you draw, I feel that you really are somebody.' Renoir missed him terribly.

Renoir himself had experienced some frightening moments in the war. He came very close to death while in the Pyrenees, suffering from a virulent form of dysentery, the course of which was prevented only by a trip to Bordeaux with Renoir's uncle. Renoir's son Jean also described an occasion on which Renoir was mistaken for a spy while painting on the Seine, saved only by a revolutionary who noticed him being taken away. Renoir had always sought out beautiful things and the war years, in which death and ugliness surrounded him, took their toll, dampening his enthusiasm and creating an apathy that was discharged only when he was taken away from its cause.

It is extraordinary that these difficult years – financial deprivation, the deaths of some of his closest friends, the end of the kind of society he grew up understanding – were never represented in his work as anything but gloriously happy, light-filled and gay. There is some evidence that Renoir actually chose to see the world as such. He looked for good things, and simply avoided anything that rocked his creative cushion. He wrote once that 'When Pissarro painted views of Paris, he always put in a funeral; I would have put in a wedding.'

Renoir held a deep nostalgia for things past, for a way of life that was simpler. Constantly recalled was his enormous dislike for technology, and he maligned contemporary society's growing dependence upon it. Much like William Morris and his Arts and Crafts movement, Renoir preached a different way of life, one where tradesmanship and pride in individual creation were more important than mass-production and the loss of aesthetic integrity it entailed. But where Morris sought to change society, to find a way of life that would encourage the traditions of the past, Renoir simply obliterated from his perspective anything that he found distasteful, offering no solution to the plights of contemporary society other than a return to the past. His art reflected that select interpretation of the world around him. In the face of much critical disclaim, public hostility and financial hardships, Renoir and his fellow painters managed to find some goodness, and they celebrated it. John House, who has written extensively on Renoir and the Impressionist school, wrote, in 'Renoir's Worlds':

> *... for many of his contemporaries the world around them was not the untroubled, smiling place that Renoir presented; Manet and Degas in painting, Zola and Maupassant in literature conceived of it very differently. Renoir's image was, as many of his associates*

Opposite:
La Loge, 1874 (Courthauld Institute, London). The painting has come to be identified with Impressionism. It was exhibited at the first Impressionist exhibition in 1874, and was, which one critic called it, 'Renoir's finest masterpiece, one of those rare paintings in which everything is a source of delight, in which everything is novel, surprising and unexpected.'

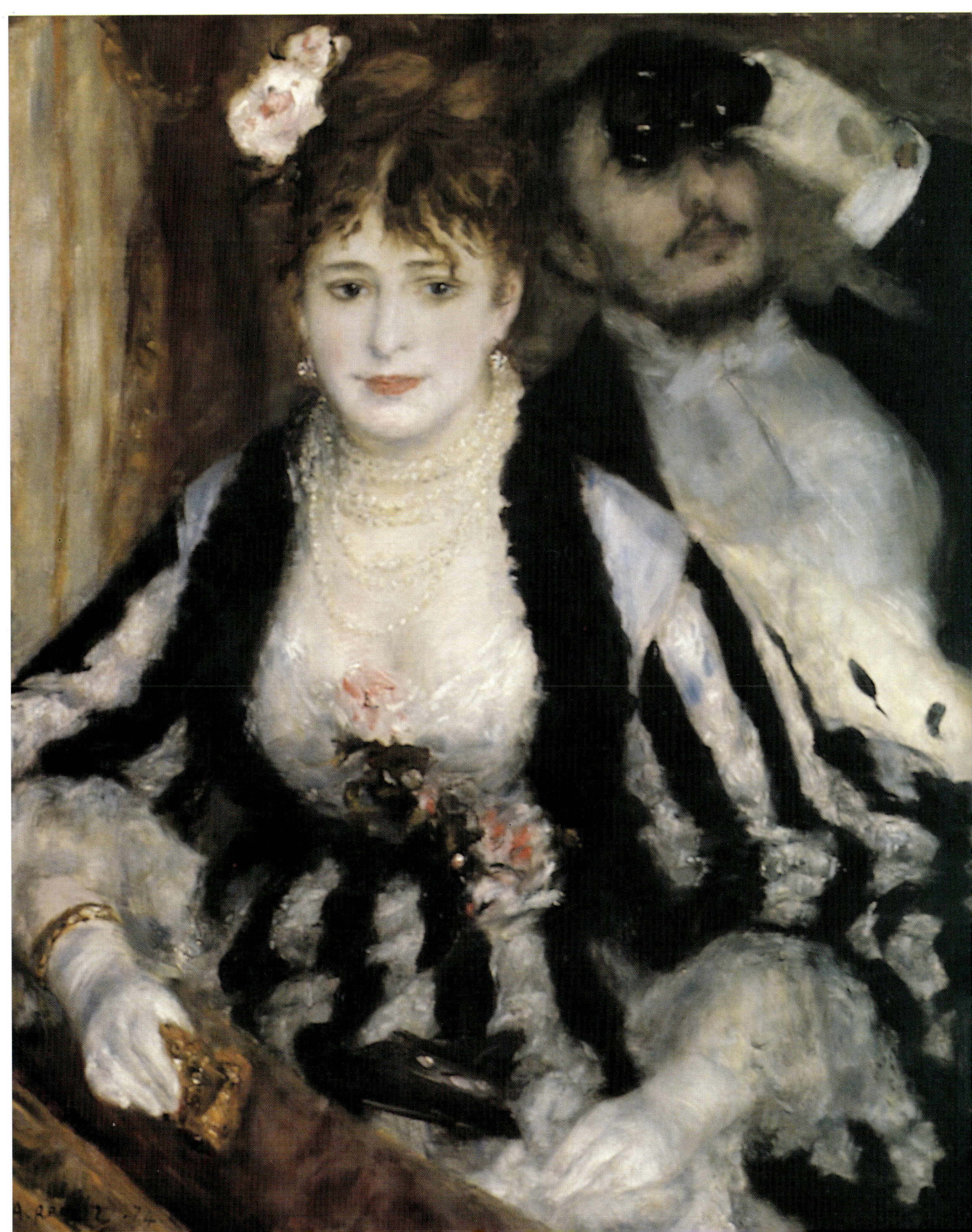

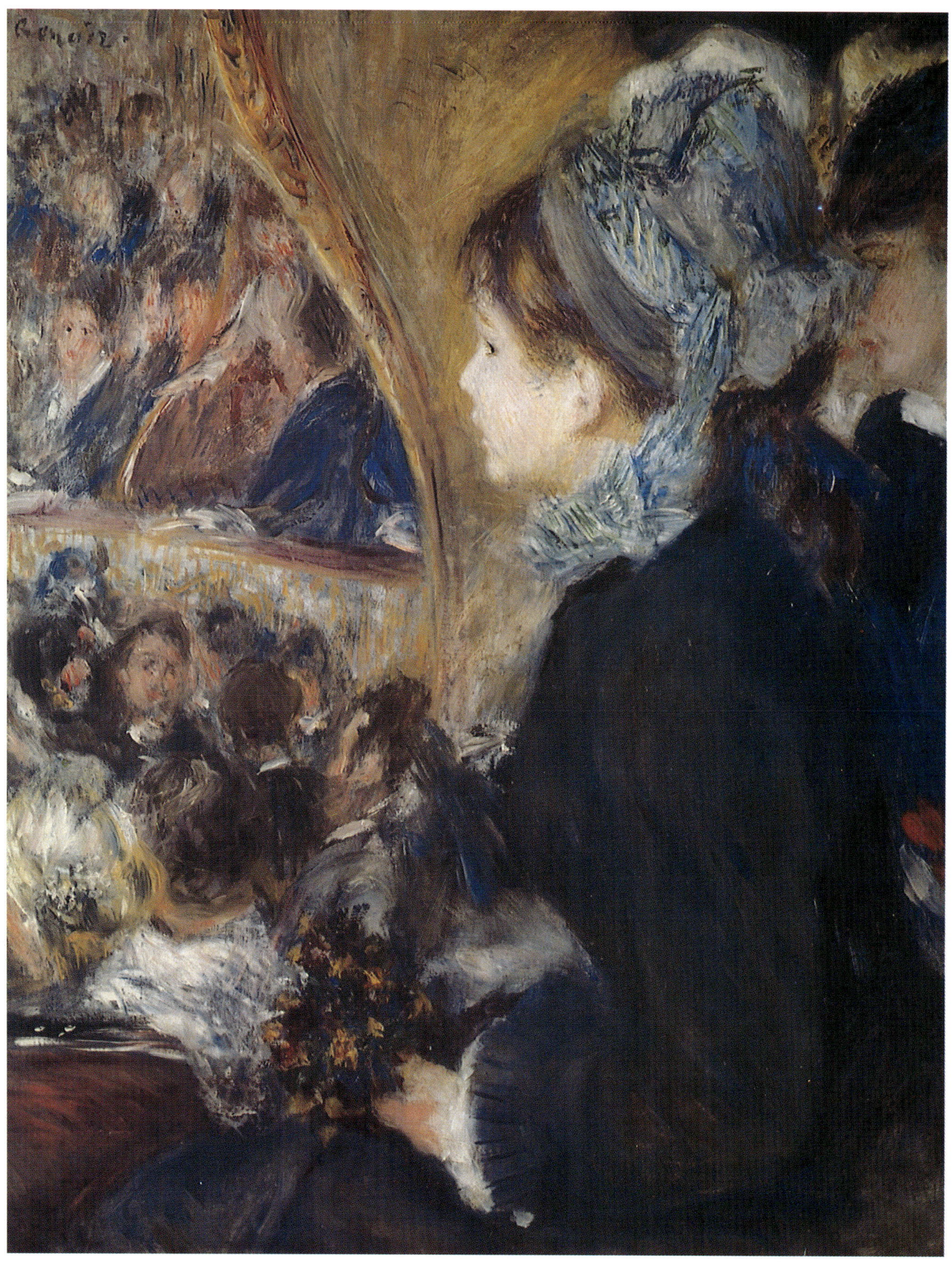

realized, both selective and edited – in what he chose to paint and how he chose to paint it. He criticized Maupassant and Zola for seeing everything black; Maupassant criticized him for seeing everything rose; Degas could not forgive him for embellishing his models. At the end of his life, Renoir could freely accept this verdict: 'One must embellish,' he told Bonnard. But within the modern-life painting of the 1870s his vision of the world was an anomaly.

The First Outing, 1875-6 (National Gallery, London). The theatre box was a common subject of Renoir's paintings in the seventies. *La Loge* had been painted a year or so earlier, to great critical acclaim, and Renoir returns here to that setting. The sitter holds a bouquet of roses, the fresh touch of nature against the rich velvets and silks of the theatre-goers' dresses.

Renoir and Monet continued to paint together after the war, particularly at Argenteuil where Monet had moved in 1872 and where they painted regattas and a number of landscapes. Monet's influence is evident in much of Renoir's work throughout that period. His paint-brush is handled with more delicacy, and his colours were lighter than ever. Monet, however, had pretty well discarded the human form, while Renoir moved in the other direction, attempting to apply Impressionist techniques to portraits, and scenes of everyday life. They argued cheerfully about the other's art. Monet ventured into figure painting for a period of time that is specifically linked to his time spent with Renoir, but he soon abandoned it in order to concentrate on land-scapes. Monet never painted the human figure well, and he said once of Renoir's landscapes, in particular about his *Bather* of 1892, 'Yes, the nude is beautiful, but see how sadly conventional the landscape is; it looks just like a photographer's decor.'

Renoir continued to submit work to the Salon, but he was consistently disappointed, and when *Riding in the Bois de Boulogne,* and *Portrait*, were rejected, he took part in the Salon des Refusés which was organized in 1873. Renoir's work met with critical acclaim at this second exhibition, but it had less prestige and did not guarantee the artist any kind of financial reward. Disillusioned, Renoir and a number of his colleagues sought an answer to the dilemma of the outdated jury system. The group of artists, which included Renoir, Monet, Bazille and Sisley, among others, had become known as the Batignolles group, and they had begun to consider the idea of yet another alternative exhibition. The war had firmly quashed any earlier such plans, but by 1874 the time seemed ripe to plan an independent exhibition aimed at those artists who painted 'nature and life in their larger realities'.

A large selection of artists were included in the exhibition, partly because the show was to be funded by the contributors themselves, and partly because the organizers felt that artists who had already achieved some critical acclaim would lend authority to the venture. Renoir suggested the name for the exhibition: *Société anonyme des artists, peintres et sculpteurs*. For a monthly subscription of five francs, artists could exhibit and sell their paintings. There would be no selection process, but there would be a committee presiding over the society, to ensure its smooth running. The first committee comprised an impressive list of names, including Pissarro, Degas, Sisley, Morisot, Guillaumin, Béliard, Renoir and Monet, among others. The exhibition was scheduled to open on 15 April, two weeks before the official Salon.

Impression, Sunrise, Monet's study of the port at Le Havre, was only one of the works he exhibited, but it was this painting which caused the group of artists to be labelled Impressionists. Louis Leroy, writing for *Le Charivari*, noted, 'Impression ... wallpaper in its embryonic state is more finished ...' The label was quickly adopted by others and within months became an accepted term in the art world. Most of the artists' contributions were either slammed or poked fun at. Renoir's *Dancer* was appreciated by some critics, but Monsieur Leroy again said that although the artist was deemed to have an appreciation of colour, he lacked the ability to draw. Renoir had also chosen *La Loge, The Parisienne, Harvesters* and three works entitled *Fleurs, Tête de Femme* and *Croquis* to exhibit, and they were surprisingly well received, in contrast to the critical attention paid to some of his colleagues. *La Loge* in particular garnered some acclaim. Painted in 1874, Renoir again adopted the subject matter of his contemporaries, in this case that of Manet. An early Impressionist painting, *La Loge* incorporated a significant amount of black, which is unusual for Renoir and indeed for the movement being represented.

In general, the few good reviews that the society received were written by journalists who had been briefed about and were sympathetic to the aims and ideals of the painters; the remainder scorned the exhibition, confused perhaps by its unique perspective and vision.

The first Impressionist exhibition was not a success in any way, but the following year, when the Salon once again rejected the works of those whom we have come to know as the great proponents of the Impressionist movement, another exhibition was launched, this time in the gallery of the art dealer Paul Durand-Ruel, an admirer of the Impressionist work and one of the few dealers to have made substantial purchases. The second exhibition was met with even greater horror, with art critics who had not bothered to cover the first show leaping into the fray. Albert Wolff, writing for the paper *Le Figaro*, said:

> *The rue Le Peletier has had bad luck. After the Opera fire here is a new disaster overwhelming the district. At Durand-Ruel's there has just opened an exhibition of so-called painting. The inoffensive passer-by attracted by the flags that decorate the facade, goes in, and a ruthless spectacle is offered to his dismayed eyes; five or six lunatics – among them a woman – a group of unfortunate creatures stricken with the mania of ambition have met here to exhibit their works. Some people burst out laughing in front of these things – my heart is oppressed by them ... These self-styled artists who call themselves 'The Intransigents' or 'The Impressionists' take a canvas, some*

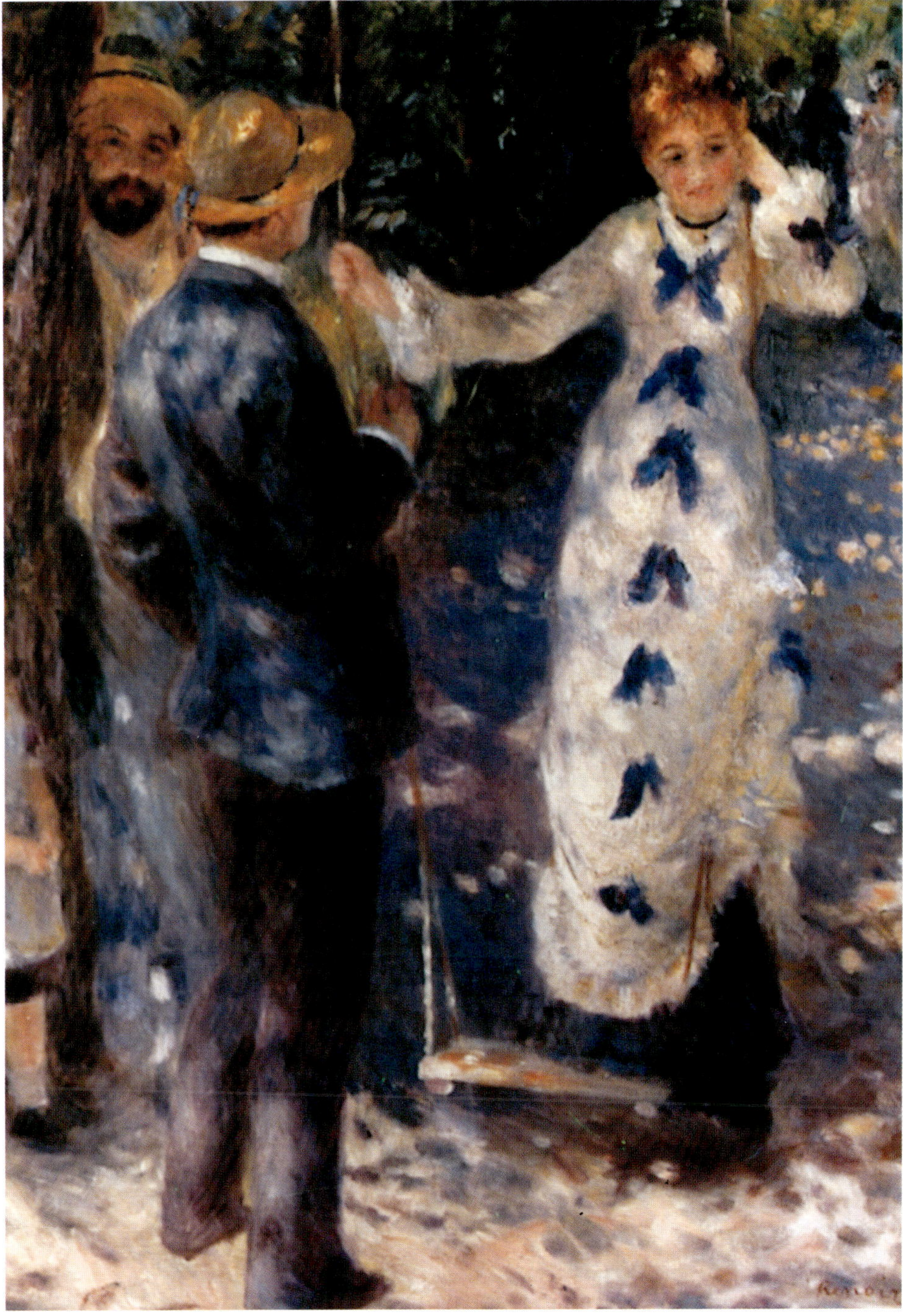

The Swing, 1876 (Musée d'Orsay, Paris). This painting was probably undertaken in the garden of Renoir's studio in the rue Cortot. Renoir attempts to render the effect of light shimmering through the trees on the dress of the model (Jeanne, a young lady from Montmartre), and its delicacy and charm make it one of his most popular works.

paint and brushes, throw some tones haphazardly on the canvas and then sign it. This is the way in which the lost souls of the Ville-Evrard [a notorious hospital for the mentally ill] pick up pebbles from the roadway, and believe that they have found diamonds.

This time Renoir was singled out for *Nude in the Sunlight*. Wolff wrote, 'Try to explain to M. Renoir that a woman's torso is not a mass of flesh in the process of decomposition with green and violet spots which denote the state of complete putrefaction of a corpse!' The painting was in fact a precursor to the classic Renoir nudes, an elegant and sensual work which embodied the Impressionist fascination with light. Quite apart from the references to putrescence, Renoir's painting was also considered unfinished and unrealistic.

By the third exhibition, however, there had come to be a body of grudging admirers; Henry James, writing for the *New York Tribune,* and Charles Bigot, in *La Révue Politique et Littéraire* were two critics who appreciated to some extent the art of the Impressionists, and understood their basic aims and characteristics.

Renoir was, nonetheless, unhappy with the labels he and his colleagues were receiving, and he refused to show with the group for several years, trying his luck again with the Salon. Renoir's painting had evolved to incorporate many of the elements which would eventually guarantee his success. At the second exhibition of Impressionists he had shown fifteen paintings, and there had been some interest from the public. Durand-Ruel had also begun to buy his work, which he had ignored in the early seventies. He was at a critical point in his career and he struggled to put on to the canvas the visions he was beginning at last to comprehend.

In 1876 Renoir rented a studio in the Rue Cortot in Montmartre, where he produced some of his most famous works, such as *Ball at the Moulin de la Galette, The Swing, Nude in Sunlight* and *Under the Arbour. The Swing* and *Le Moulin de la Galette* were painted simultaneously in the garden of his studio; he painted *The Swing* in the mornings and the *Le Moulin* in the afternoons. Both paintings belie the firm grasp of Impressionism Renoir had achieved; the effect of light on his scenes is exquisitely rendered, redolent with the charm that would make his work so accessible and popular. The subject matter of both paintings was modern, a foray from the staid Salon-type paintings that Renoir had been accustomed to painting. In his garden at the rue Cortot, Renoir created a kind of pastoral world that fed his imagination, and challenged his perspectives. He surrounded himself with nature in the same way that he had surrounded himself with the paintings of the masters as a child. He sought inspiration there; used nature as his study.

Many of the Impressionists, among them Renoir's closest friends, had left Paris in search of the nature they longed to paint. Pissarro moved to Pointoise and then to Eragney. Caillebotte and Monet found solace in their gardens at Petit-Gennevilliers and Giverny. Renoir alone chose to remain in Paris, but he had found a stunning and overgrown sanctuary in his garden at Montmartre. Jean Renoir, in *Renoir, My Father,* wrote:

> *The house in the rue Cortot was falling to pieces but Renoir did not mind. It provided the advantage of a large garden, with a*

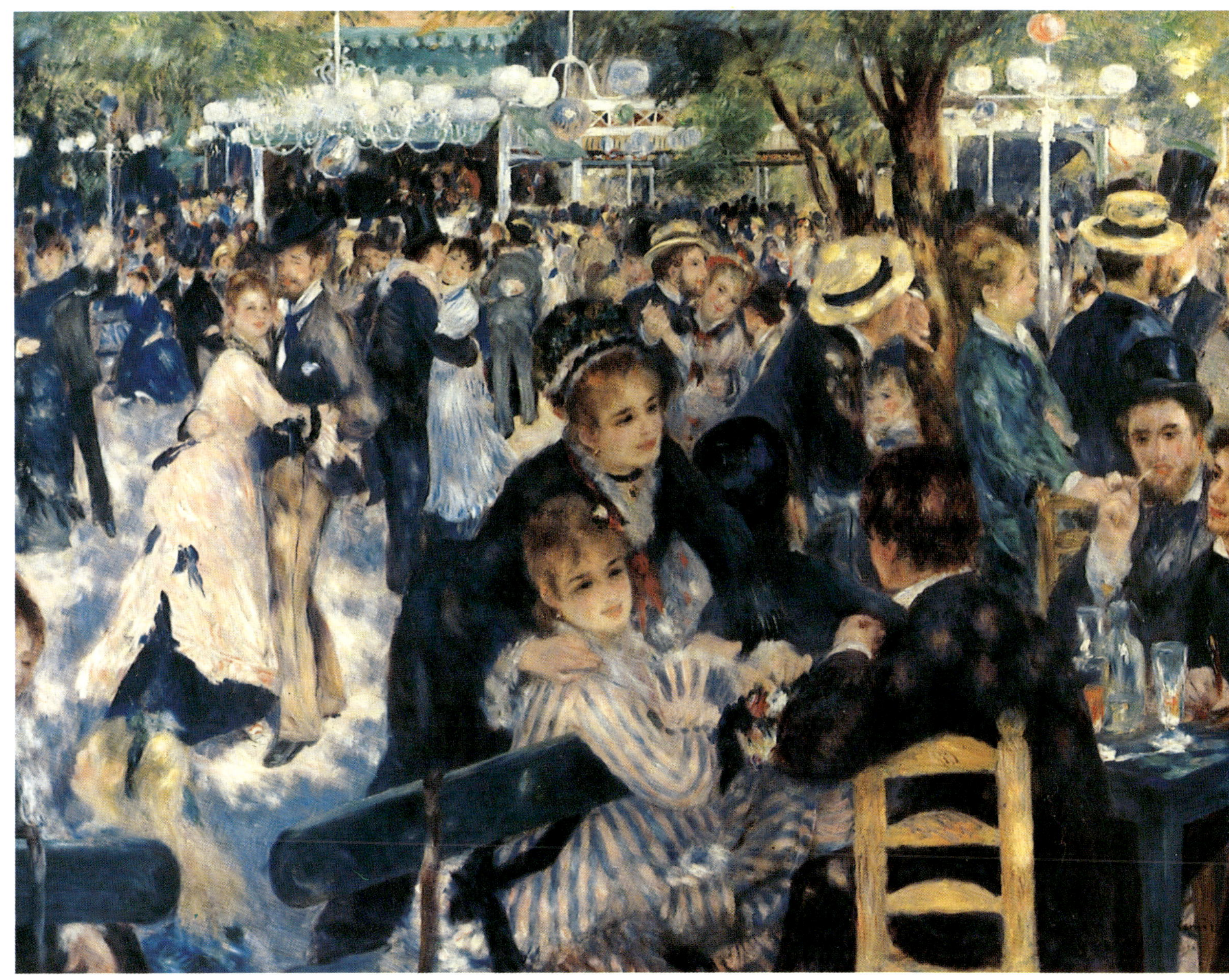

magnificent view of the countryside as far as Saint-Denis. A mysterious stately garden, like Zola's paradou – *what was once part of a fine residence.*

The studio was indeed part of a private park which had belonged to an eighteenth-century château, and it allowed Renoir a taste of country life among the society of Paris.

It was a society to which Renoir had finally been accepted. In the later part of the seventies, Renoir met and became friendly with the publisher Georges Charpentier, who hosted an exclusive and impressive salon. Charpentier was taken with Renoir and his work, and the painter was invited to the Charpentier family's social events, where he met many of the leading literary and artistic figures of the day.

Ball at the Moulin de la Galette, 1876 (Musée d'Orsay, Paris). This work was painted on the spot at the famous dance hall at the top of the Butte Montmartre. Renoir painted it at the same time as *The Swing*, and both were recognized as works of great genius. There is a similarity between this painting and *La Grenouillère;* Renoir was an unsurpassed documenter of the popular crowd scenes of French café society.

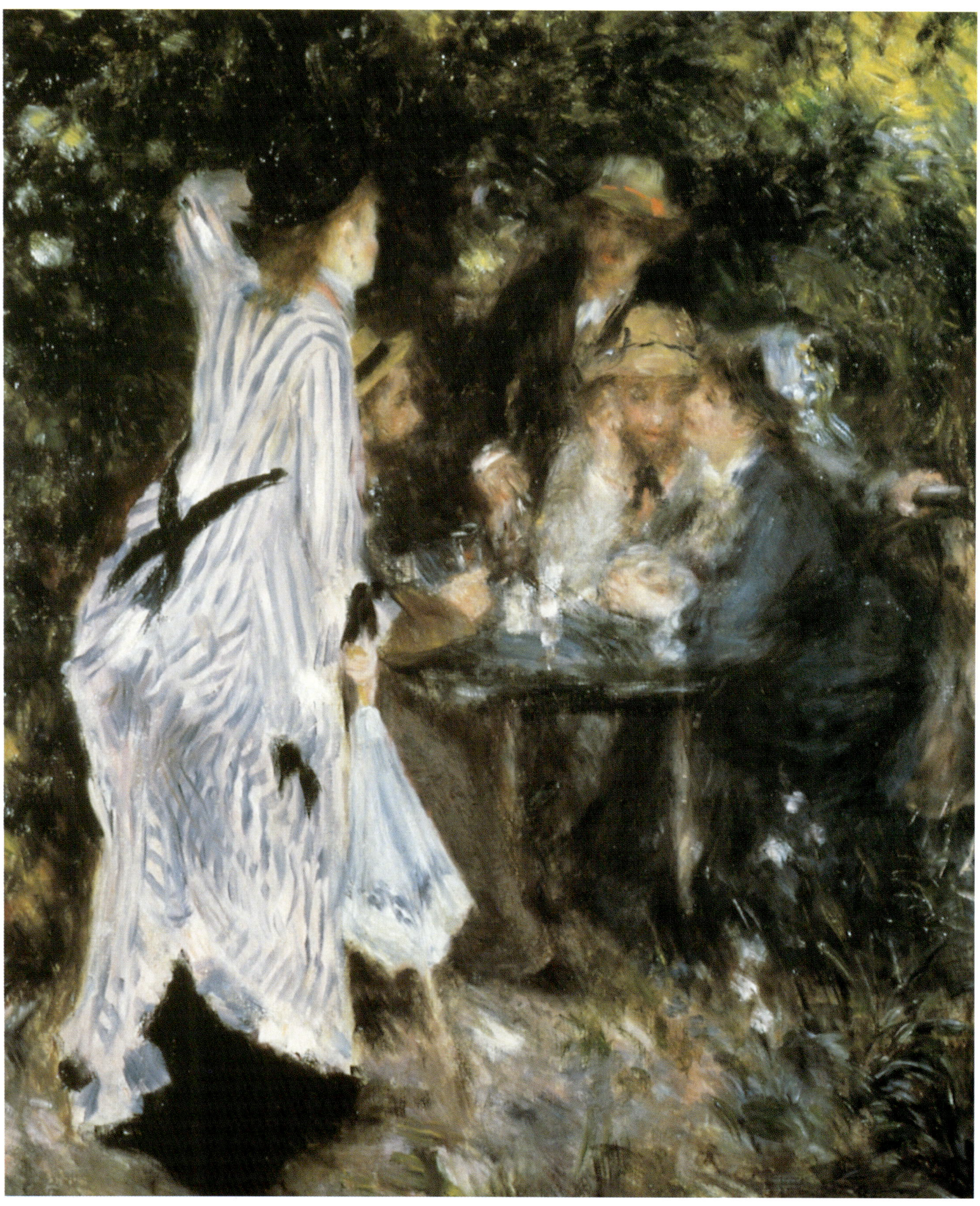

Renoir was still a man of simple tastes and manners; in fact, that would not ever change, despite the success he gained in later years. He found himself a member of a group of glittering individuals, many of whom were talented, interesting and intellectual; most of whom were rich and poised. Renoir gained dozens of portrait commissions through this circle, and this became his livelihood. While he spent much of his time in this society, it is not clear whether or not he felt at home. It has been suggested that he played the role of eccentric entertainment for the guests. He also became friendly with Paul Bérard, a wealthy patron who enjoyed the relationship specifically because of Renoir's lack of artifice. John House, in 'Renoir's Worlds', noted:

> *In his personal manners, Renoir made absolutely no attempt to conform with the norms of fashionable society. The greedy table manners and nervous tic which amused Bérard greatly offended the mother of Jacques-Emile Blanche. On one occasion, he forgot to put on his dress coat for a formal dinner with the Charpentiers; his notorious absent-mindedness even found its place in contemporary gossip columns.*

Renoir appears to have been extremely self-absorbed. While his paintings are social extravaganzas, dancing with colour, light and a vibrancy that is enticing, evocative and festive, his character was not that of a robust, happy man. Renoir was highly strung, restless and demanding. He thrust his emotions and every aspect of his life back into his painting, often ignoring those around him, and the very importance of that work. He constantly changed his mind, blustering with confidence one moment, and exhibiting his deep-rooted insecurity the next. Some say that he saw the world around him as a dark and depressing place and felt strongly that art should be an escape from the harsh realities that existed around them all. He chastized his friend Monet for depicting society so accurately, preferring instead the decorative and optimistic works of the Rococo painters.

He constantly changed his mind and preferred to move from rented studio or house to the homes of his friends rather than purchasing any tangible security or setting down roots. De Wyzewa, in his diary, noted that Renoir 'has in his blood an unfortunate need for change ...' Those kinder to the artist say that his restlessness and dissatisfaction are only reflections of the fact that he was a painter through and through; anything second to that must have appeared to him to be a waste of energy. He travelled to find new inspiration, a new perspective; he made new friends to increase the extent of his world, but it is likely that he did so mainly in the name of his art.

But perhaps for financial reasons, or perhaps because he enjoyed becoming a part of society that had previously eluded both him and

Under the Arbour, Moulin de la Galette, 1876 (Pushkin Museum, Moscow). Like Renoir's other paintings of this lively dance hall, down the road from his home in Montmartre, this work reflects perfectly the jolly and slightly eccentric atmosphere.

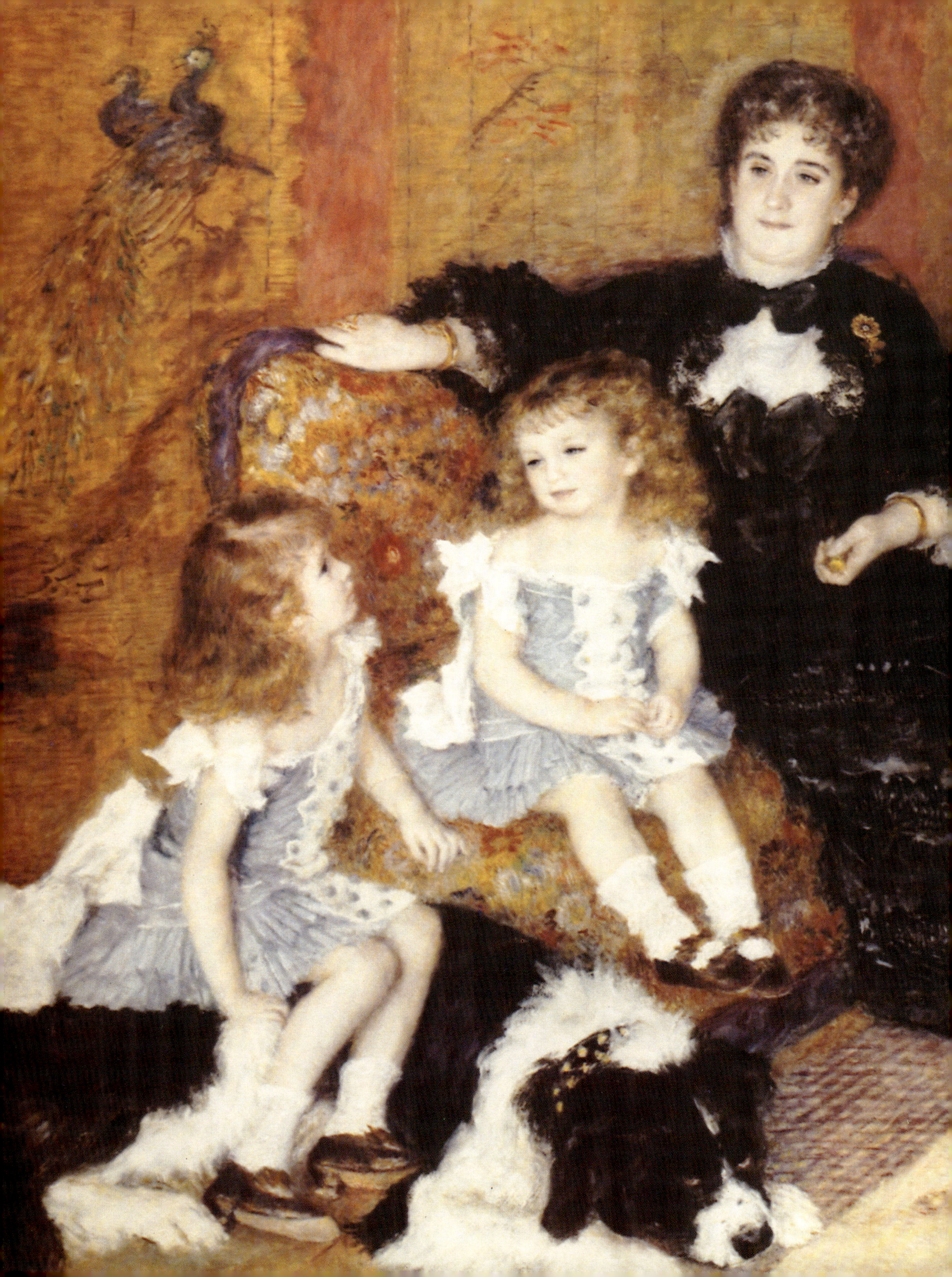

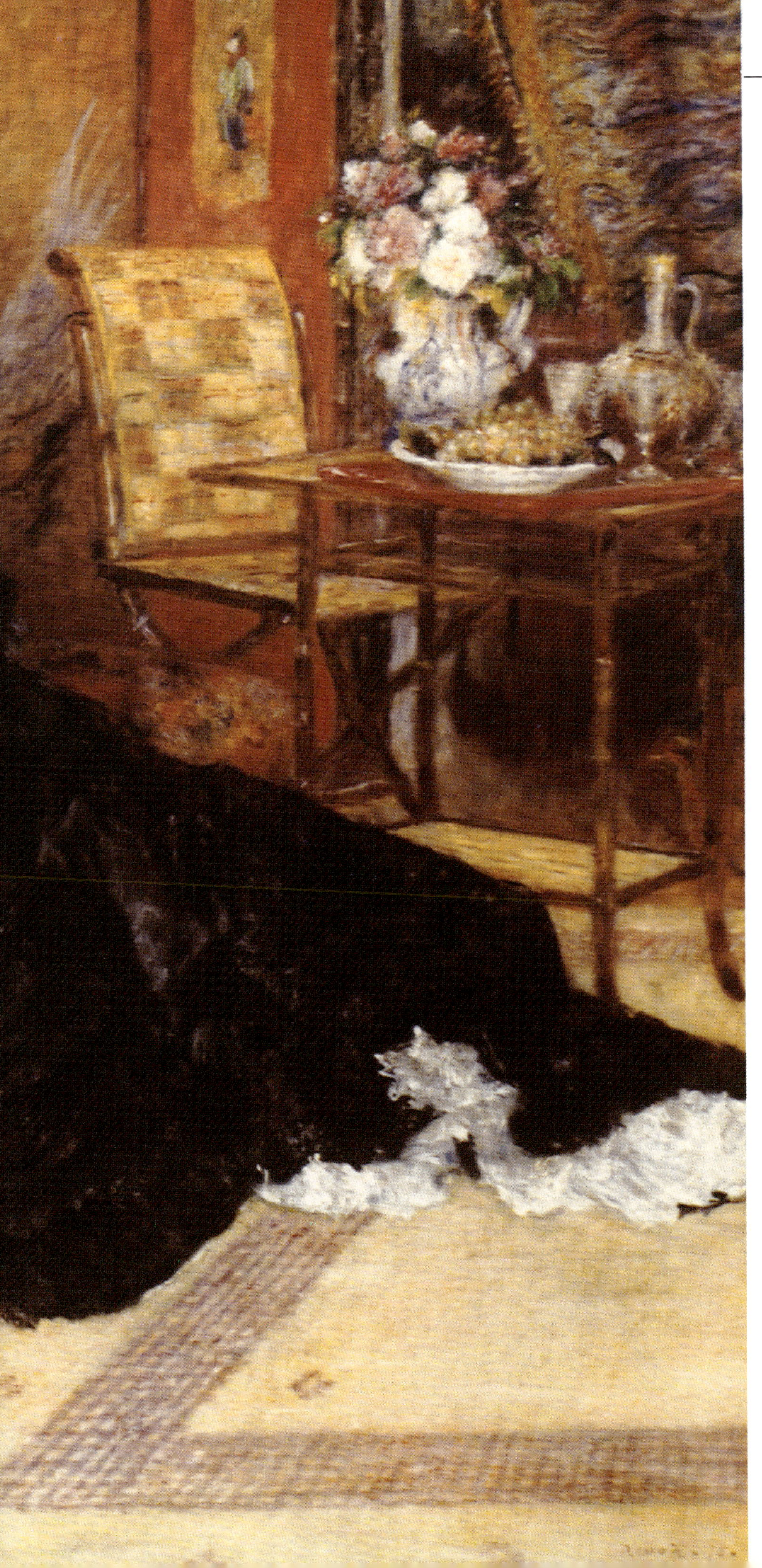

Portrait of Madame Charpentier and her Children, 1878 (Metropolitan Museum of Art, New York). This painting assured Renoir success at the 1879 Salon, making him a celebrity in the literary and political circle of the Charpentiers, who were flushed with the accomplishment of the work. The grouping is keenly rendered, and the flesh tones of the children in particular unparalleled in contemporary art.

A Box at the Opera, 1880 (Clark Art Institute, Williamstown). Curiously similar to *La Loge*, which had attracted a great deal of critical acclaim, this painting was not shown at the Salon, but its technical mastery and sympathy with Renoir's contemporary works would likely have guaranteed its success. The flowers are a traditional Renoir touch; he loved bouquets of tight roses and used them on a number of occasions.

his family, he did humour the circles of the art dealers, many of whom became close friends. His effortless simplicity made him popular with people of all classes; he was not interested in material comforts, or in vast sums of money. He wished for success because he believed in his art; he required money in order to live, and painting was not an easy career to support for one of modest means.

Paul Durand-Ruel in particular was a good friend to Renoir and to the Impressionists. He believed in their vision and he staked a good deal of his personal fortune on them. Renoir never forgot the favours afforded him by this generous man. He told his son Jean, 'Without him we couldn't have survived.' Durand-Ruel bought dozens of Renoir's paintings and sketches, allowing him to continue to work and encouraging his art. Another collector, Victor Choquet, helped the struggling painter, and Renoir was able to concentrate on his art, with the support of these men of unusual vision and beneficence.

Renoir's less than officious experiences with the Impressionist exhibitions led him back to the Salon in 1878. *The Cup of Coffee* was accepted, and the following year *Portrait of Madame Charpentier and her Children*, and *Portrait of Mlle Jeanne Samary* were also chosen. His work was celebrated within the hallowed halls of the art establishment, but outside that the public had still failed to come to grips with the Impressionist vision.

The portrait of Madame Charpentier and her two children illustrated the new maturity of Renoir's work. He indulged his love of sensuous, rich colours and in an informal and lighthearted composition he created an extraordinarily flattering likeness of his new friend's wife and children. Renoir was desperate to make a good impression upon the society in which portrait painters could make a healthy living. He emulated to some extent the successful techniques of John Singer Sargent, drawing attention to the popular oriental props and over-emphasizing the grandeur of the setting. But his subjects fail to succumb to the formula. They lived and breathed in what appears to be a very stultified existence; their skin is fresh and wholesome.

There was no doubt that Renoir's paintings were remarkable. On the strength of *Madame Charpentier* and several other significant works, commissions for his portraits poured in; it was clear that the subjects of these works enjoyed being the focus of such an abundantly evident expression of joy. His paintings sing with life; his paintbrush caressing its subjects intimately. Light touches a bosom here, a half-smile is emphasized; any slight imperfections are swept away. It is an interesting paradox that Renoir sought to celebrate imperfection as the fundamental facet of beauty, yet he did not hesitate to embellish here, delete there, in order to preserve the appearance he wished to create. It is likely that he genuinely saw things in the way he painted them and it

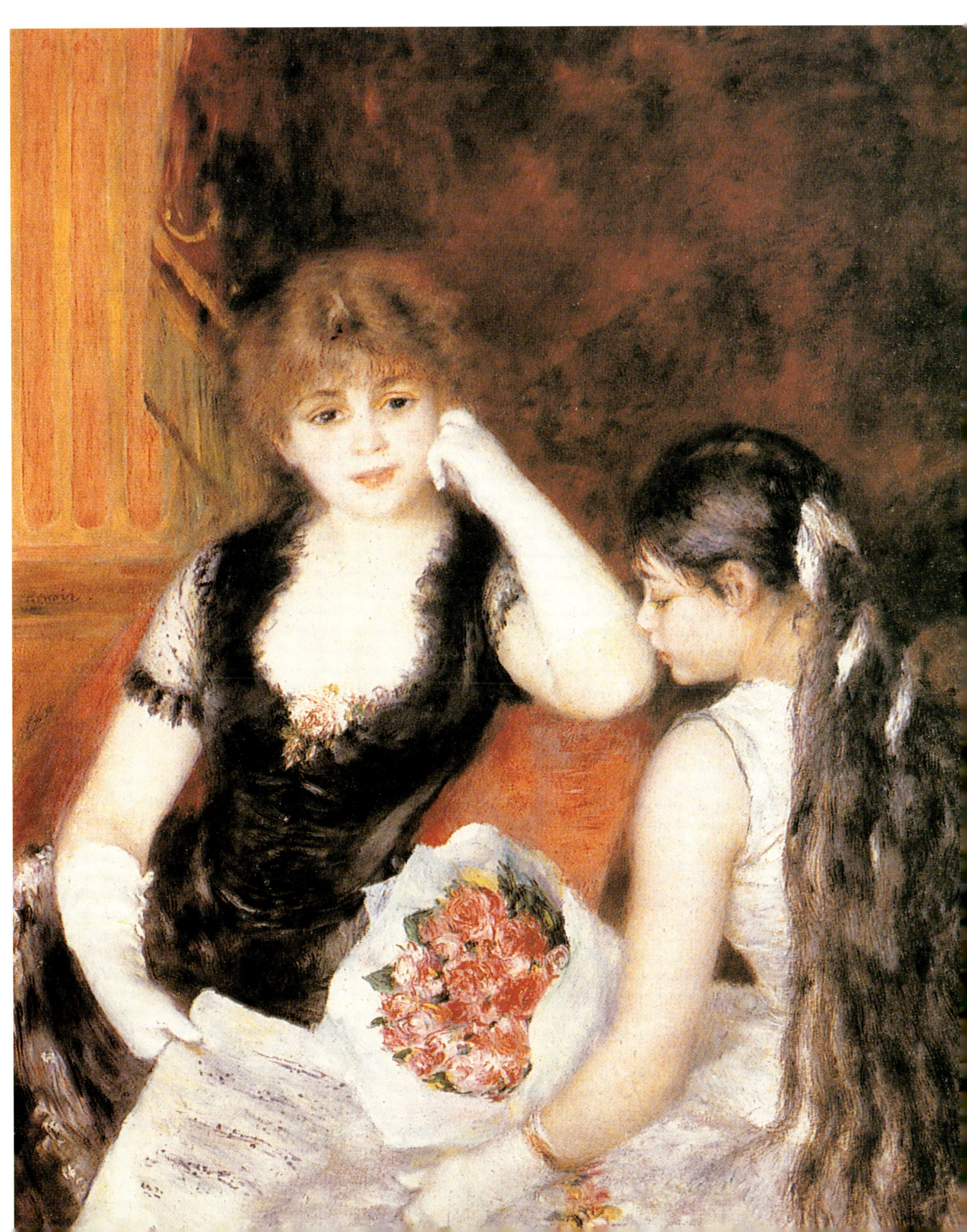

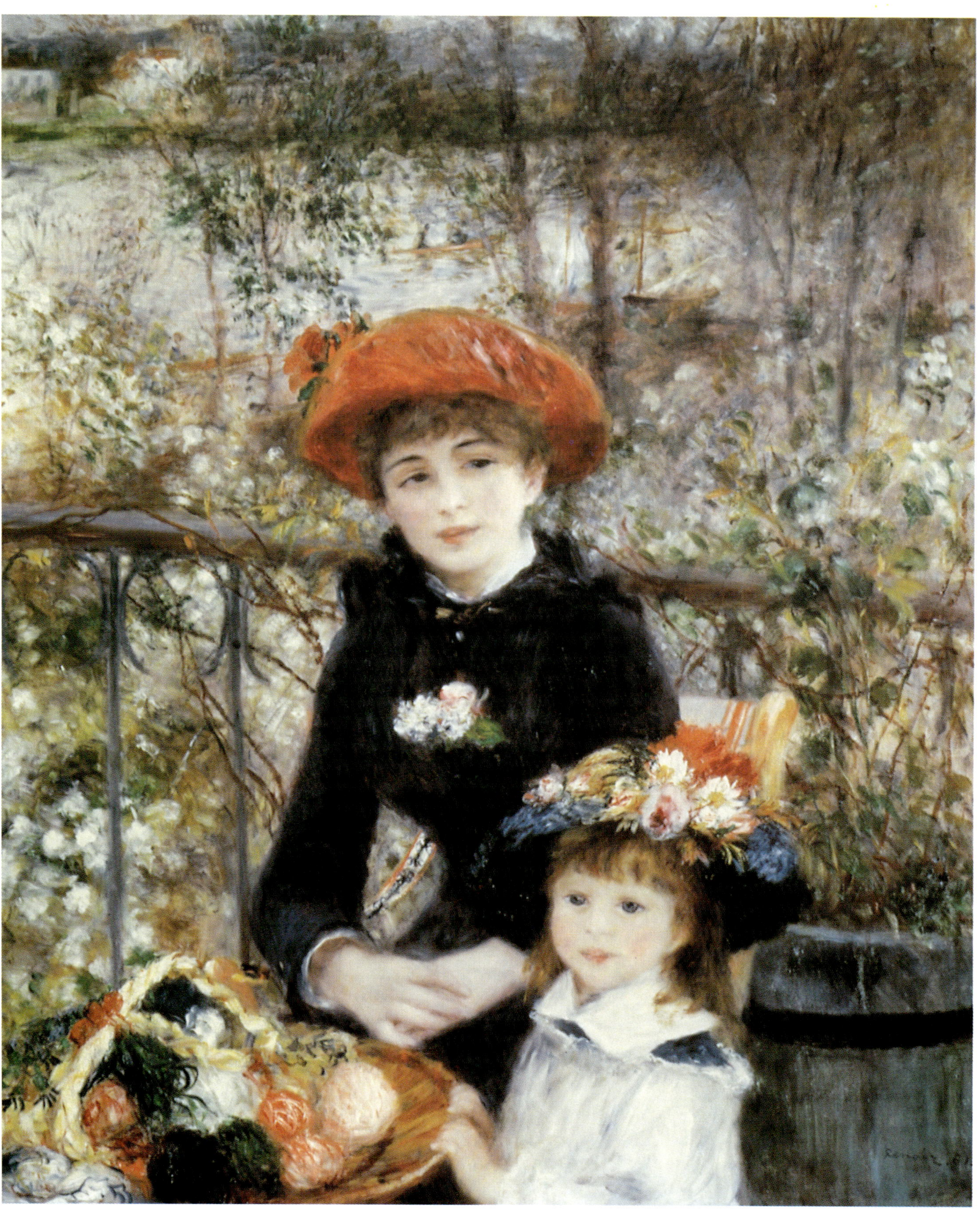

has been said that more people were converted to Impressionism by Renoir's portraits than by any other single means.

The seventies was a decade of increasing success for Renoir. His talents were enriched by the growing objectives of the Impressionists, which he cheerfully applied to all of his works - landscapes, nudes, portraits, café scenes alike. His studio at Montmartre was a hive of activity, becoming the central meeting place for his ever-widening circle of acquaintances. He was one of the few artists among this circle to have achieved some financial success, and because he had neither dependants nor responsibilities, he was able to live quite happily on what he earned. His studio was just down the road from the Moulin de la Galette, an open-air dance hall situated at the base of the windmill from which it took its name. Renoir rented his studio nearby specifically to paint the happy scenes that characterized the venue, and his famous painting *Ball at the Moulin de la Galette* was painted on the spot.

Until this time Renoir had concentrated on families, or individual dancers, or isolated groups of figures, as in La Grenouillère. But the Moulin de la Galette sparked his imagination. Renoir loved the excitement and frivolity that distinguished this Parisian hall. *Ball at the Moulin de la Galette*, is pure Renoir - radiant colours, throngs of festive merrymakers, twirling and gay on the dance floor, with mid-summer light shining on their faces. It took him six months to complete this painting, and he returned night after night in order to paint real-life dancers. He refused to work anywhere other than in situ, although there is some evidence that he worked from sketches as well, and in this painting he was generous with the splashes of dappled bright colour and light that were to become his trademarks. The party was sketched on to unprimed canvas and he lost the earth tones of his earlier works, replacing them with vibrant blues and soft musty greys that made so real the effects of the light in the open air.

Renoir loved to paint life as he saw it, slightly messy, gay and sincere, full of light, and relaxed, happy people. Whether Renoir genuinely believed that these joyous gatherings reflected accurately the lives of the merrymakers, or whether he resolutely painted what he wanted to see is unknown. He had seen the horrors of war, had lived in poverty in the slums of Paris. His ability to find goodness is remarkable. John House noted:

> *In the world around him, as an interviewer noted in 1892, Renoir felt a 'horror at its tormented aspects ... He loves everything that is joyous, brilliant and consoling in life'. Sometimes he claimed that the world was so pleasant a place; he told Julie Manet that 'in the past when he frequented the Moulin de la Galette, he noticed how many delicate feelings there were among the people whom Zola depicted as appalling.' He remembered how, in the dazzling*

On the Terrace, 1881 (Chicago Institute of Art). An idyllic shot of mother and child, the relationships between whom Renoir found an overwhelming fascination. The setting is the Seine at Chatou, and while the composition expresses a certain timeless elegance, Renoir has not yet adopted the classical technique that would bury for many years the energy and life of his Impressionist style.

> *sunlight of Algiers, the sordid rags of a beggar came to look like a royal robe of gold ... Such a transformation was not just the result of the southern sun; it reflected his personal quest for a surface beauty which transcended human suffering.*

The painting became Renoir's acknowledged masterpiece, and the pleasure he obviously realized from creating it spills from every inch of the canvas. Other paintings fulfilled this promise and Renoir's gift for creating life on a two-dimensional canvas became legendary.

About this time Renoir met Aline Charigot, a seamstress of peasant origin who became his lover and companion. Lise Tréhot had married the architect George Briere de l'Isle in April of 1871, and Renoir, despite a string of unimportant liaisons, was lonely. Aline had come to Paris from Essoyes in Champagne to find work, and from that time she regularly appeared in his paintings, slipping easily into the place of Lise. The young Aline was fresh-faced and beautiful in an unadventurous way. She appears in the foreground of *The Luncheon of the Boating Party*, as a pert, slightly plump and certainly pleasing young woman. For a man who took little notice of class differences, it is puzzling that he kept Aline tucked carefully away from the clutches of his society friends.

Perhaps he felt distanced from them, felt that for them he was merely court jester. Maybe he viewed his personal life as something separate from the life he shared with the acquaintances he had made in these circles. But he had befriended many of them to such an extent that he upheld regular correspondence, and it is surprising to learn that none of them was aware of the existence of Aline until she and their six-year-old son Pierre were brought to meet Berthe Morisot, married to Manet's brother Eugène, in 1891.

Aline was considered ungainly by the members of Renoir's fashionable set, a distinct disadvantage to the popular artist. But Renoir's paintings of her belie a gentle warmth and honesty. She had put on a great deal of weight since the early days of their association, but Renoir painted her as often in her adipose state as he did when she was merely plump, so it is unlikely that he found her any less beautiful, or indeed an embarrassment. In much of his later work she came to represent a rich, earthy goodness, creating for Renoir a comfortable nest from which he was able to fly when he felt the urge, but to which he was always glad to return. His life of wealth and gaiety contrasted greatly with the simple pastoral existence he shared with Aline, and even his increasing financial success and critical acclaim failed to change their unaffected lifestyle.

Still, Renoir's new contentment was unable to quell the escalating disquiet he was feeling. In 1881 Renoir left Paris for Algiers, where he sought peace from his increasingly confusing double existence. He was

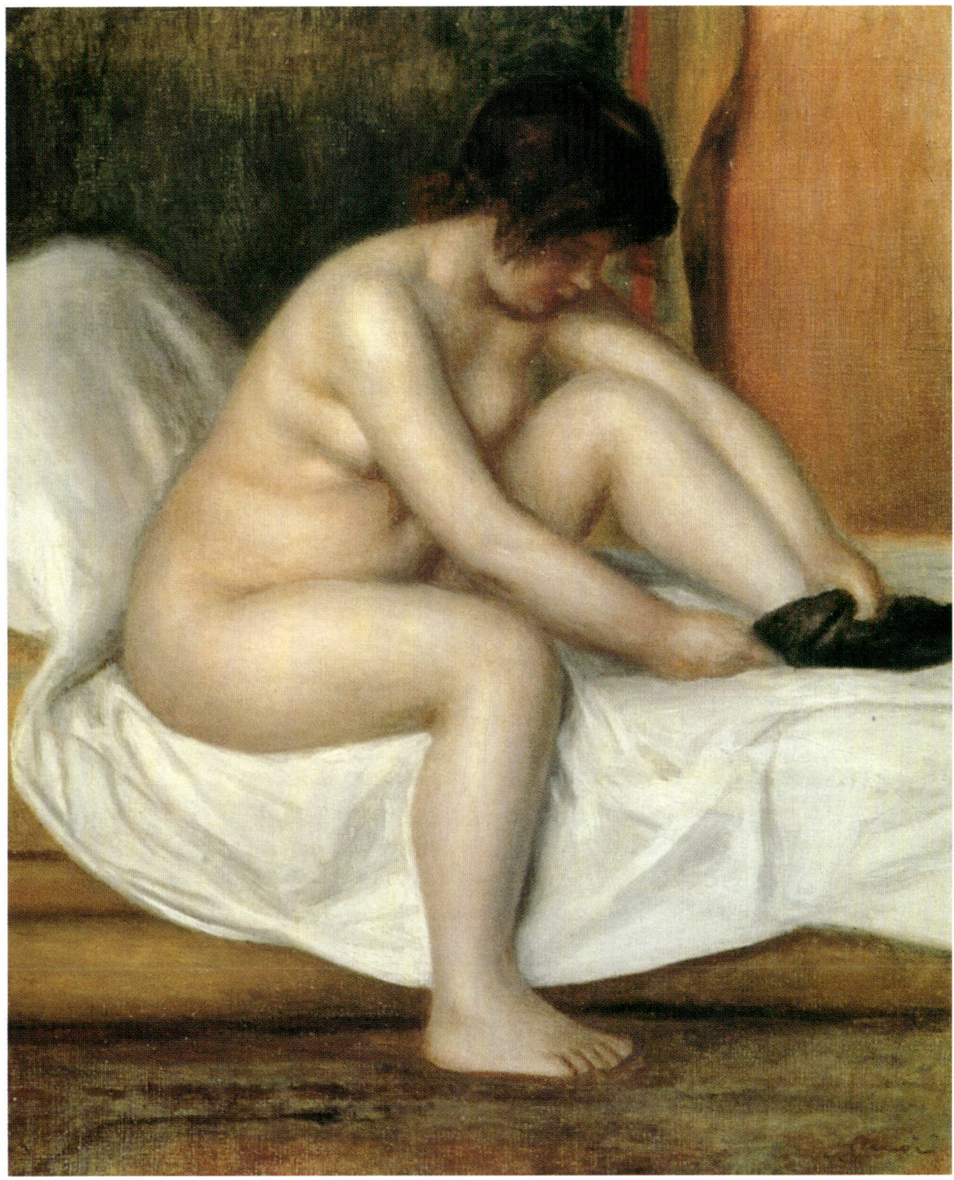

Nude, *c.* 1885 (Philadelphia Museum of Art). A robust and glowing nude, this painting exhibits the classical influence on Renoir's figures. The influence of the pearly period is not yet evident, but the nudes painted in this period are less idealistic and celebratory. They are studies, it seems, for Renoir's growing understanding of the female form.

deeply tired by the whirlwind social life he experienced with the Paris set, as well as the growing number of commissions that sprung from it, and it must also have been a strain to maintain what appears to have been a completely separate yet full life with Aline.

He returned after several weeks, having painted a number of rich and vividly coloured landscapes and scenes of Algerian women. Back in France, however, he suffered a breakdown and left a few months later for Italy, in order to rest. It was no accident that he chose Italy; it held the answer to a personal crisis that would haunt him for the next ten years.

CHAPTER 3

Crises and Conflict

'When I look back at my life I compare it to one of those corks thrown into the river. Off it goes, then it is drawn into an eddy, pulled back, plunges and rises, is caught by a grass, makes desperate efforts to get free and ends by losing itself, I do not know where ...'

Renoir

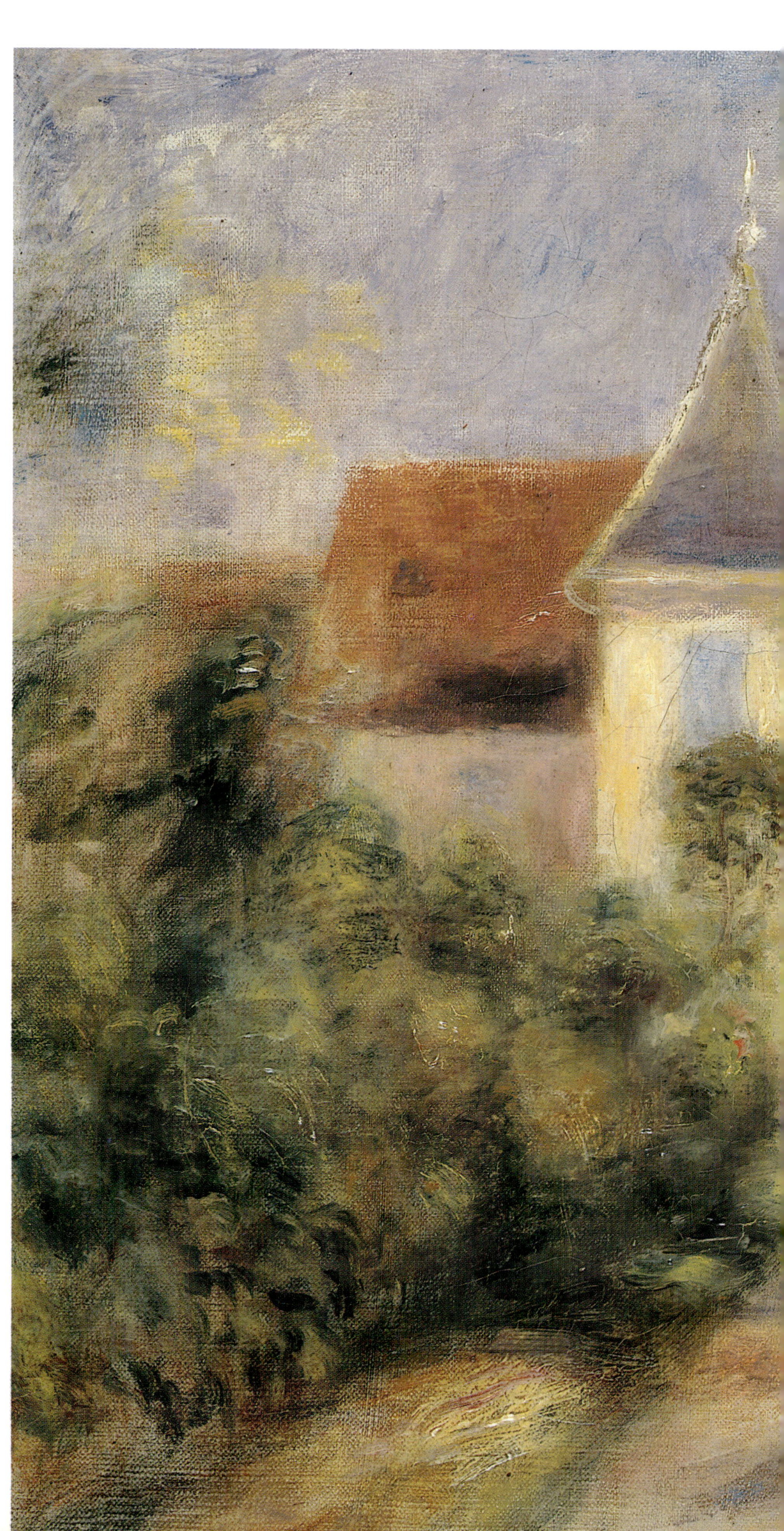

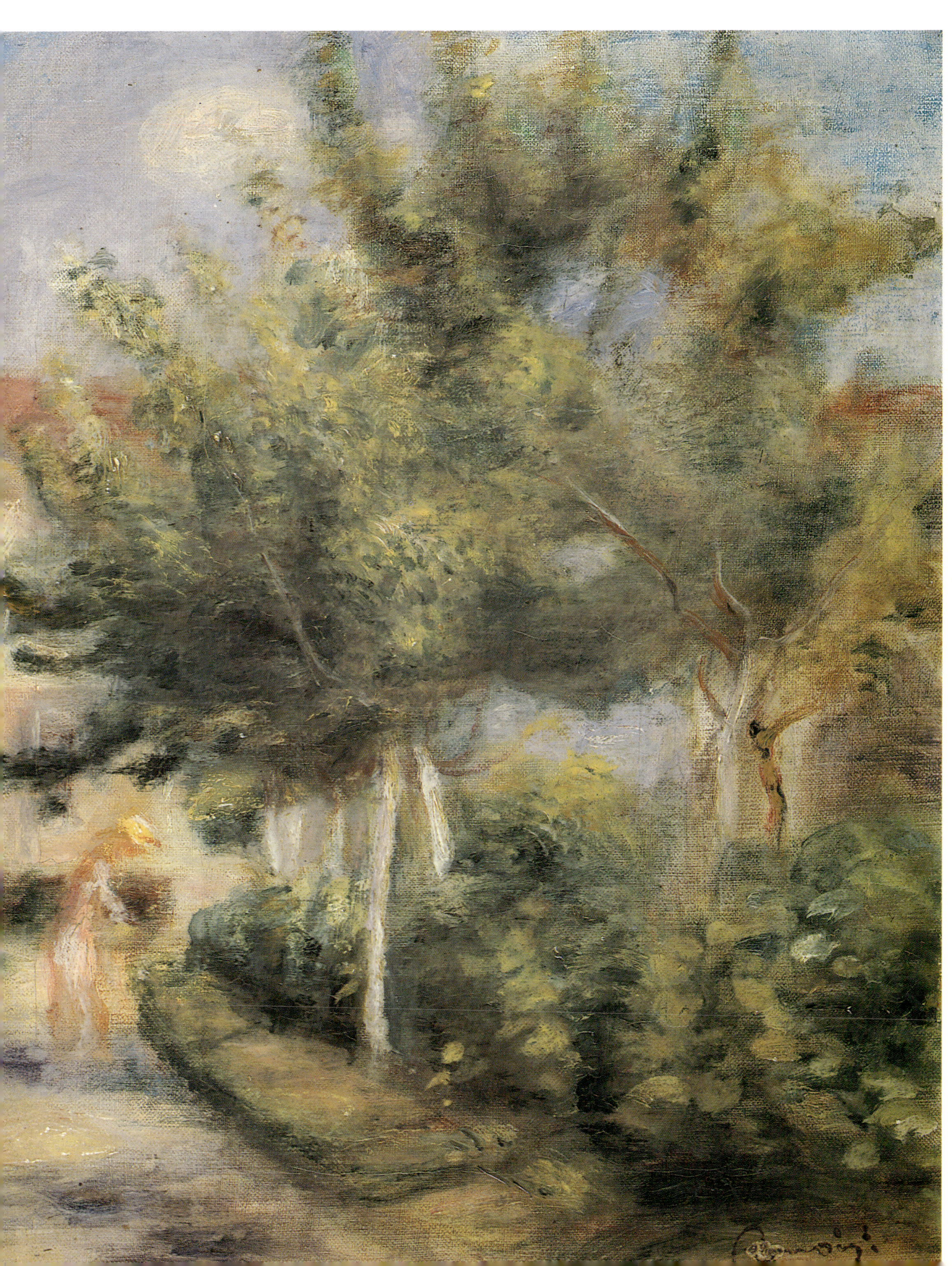

Overleaf:
Renoir's House at Essoyes, 1906 (Private collection). Essoyes was the village of his wife Aline's birth. Renoir grudgingly bought his first house here, chosen by Aline and 'a house that he does not want to buy'. Nevertheless, the couple spent many happy summers here, and they went on to buy another home in Cagnes.

The eighties marked a time of change for Renoir; it was a period of near constant experimentation, one of dissatisfaction and creative dilemmas. Yet curiously it was a period of enormous personal contentment.

In 1885 Aline Charigot gave birth to Renoir's first son Pierre, and his life became ordered, supremely happy, and rich with the emotion that had previously eluded him. Yet strangely enough it was in this atmosphere of warmth and security that Renoir experienced his *periode aigre*, the 'dry' or 'harsh' period that changed the nature of his art. His trip to Italy in 1881 had been a search for classical traditions. His splendid *Luncheon of the Boating Party* had been painted earlier that summer, and it reflected Renoir's growing need for structure and more refined composition. He was less content to suggest, seeking instead definition and statement. He was alarmed to discover that if he'd ever acquired them, he'd now lost all conventional skills of drawing and form.

In Italy he was drawn to the work of Raphael and the influence on his ideology and approach was immediate, if only slowly incorporated into his work. He wrote from Italy:

> *I have been to see the Raphaels in Rome. They are wonderful and I should have seen them before. They are full of knowledge and wisdom. Unlike me he did not seek the impossible. But it's beautiful.*

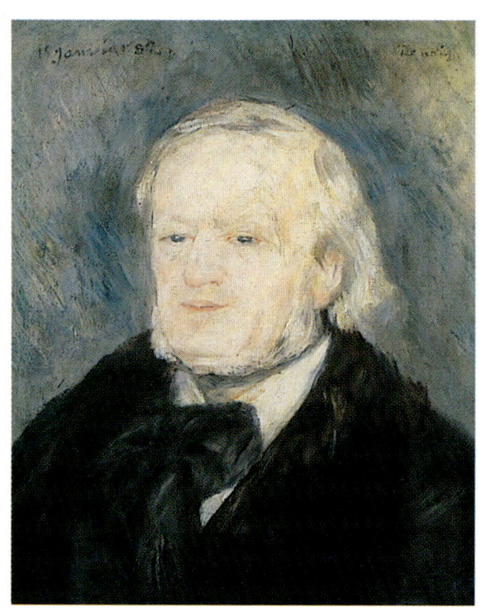

Richard Wagner, (Musée d'Orsay, Paris). Wagner graciously allowed Renoir to paint him, but the result was a surprising disappointment. The portrait reveals little of the composer's personality; its colours are flat.

His style would alter dramatically; he paid considerably more attention to composition and drawing than he did to colour, and for some time his work lost its appealing sensuality and spontaneity. From Italy he visited Sicily where his request to paint the great composer Wagner was accepted. Clearly daunted by the magnitude of the task, and lacking the confidence of his earlier style, the painting is empty of life and indeed any kind of insight into the character of the great man. Wagner himself said, 'I look like a Protestant minister', clearly disappointed with Renoir's interpretation. Renoir's portraiture had always been robust, paying tribute to its subjects and often imbibing them with new life. The Wagner says little.

But not all of this new work held such little promise, reflecting so clearly his melancholy outlook. His changing style is evident in his work *The Umbrellas,* which marks most poignantly Renoir's departure from Impressionist technique to the much more sedate, linear classicism that was to characterize his *periode aigre*. The right-hand side of the painting was painted in the early part of the decade (1881-2), and illustrates his much more decorative, pointillist technique. The left-hand side, painted towards the end of his dry period, illustrates the sharply contoured style of his new work.

Opposite:
The Umbrellas, 1881-5 (National Gallery, London). One of Renoir's most important works, this painting reflects the change in style that occurred throughout his dry period. The right-hand side of the painting is evidently Impressionist in technique, the left shows the new classical influence.

Throughout Renoir's dry period he virtually ceased to paint scenes from everyday life in France, producing portraits and still-lifes

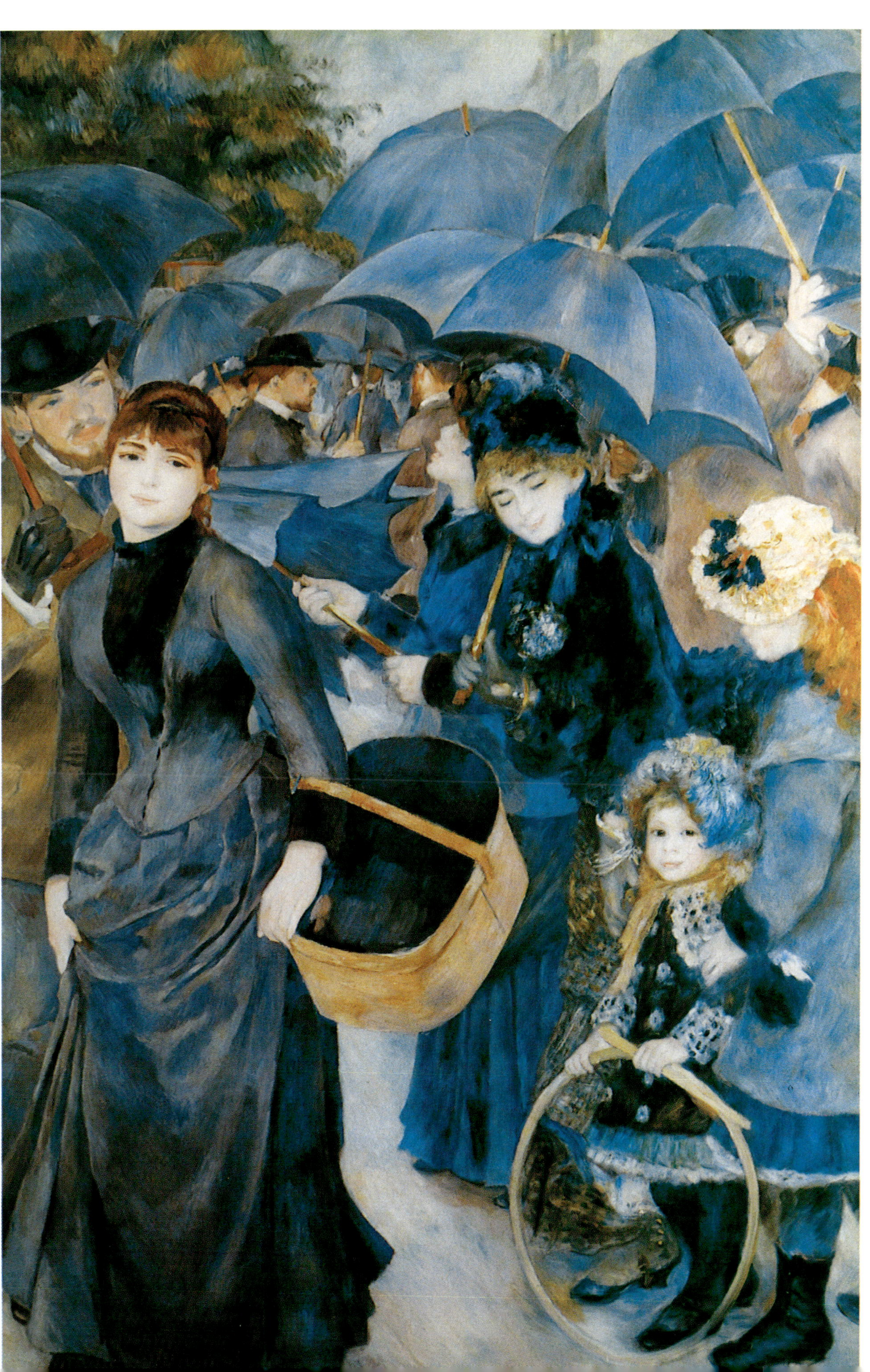

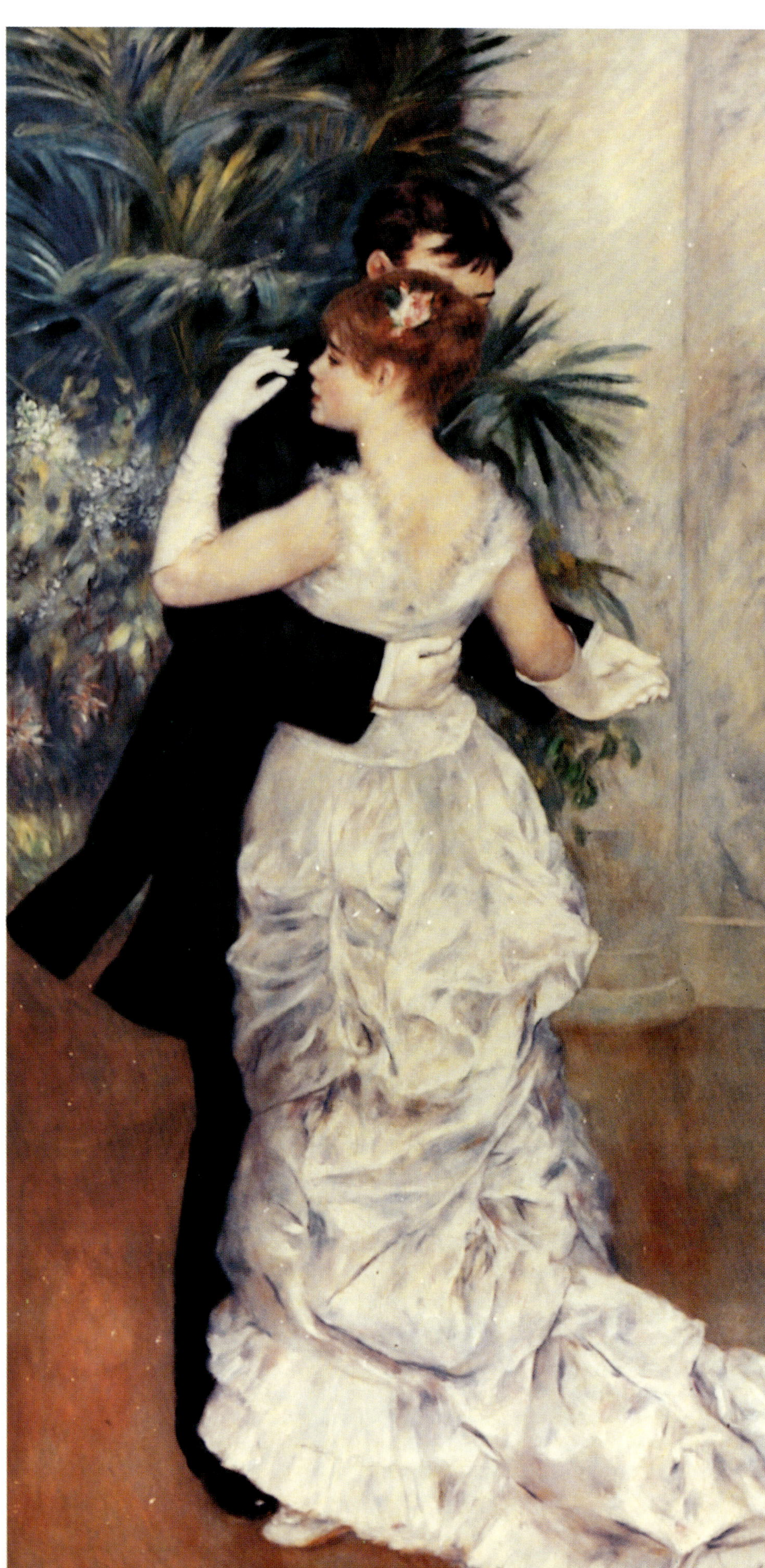

Dance in the City, 1883 (Musée d'Orsay, Paris). The *Dance* series of paintings was commissioned by art dealer and friend Paul Durand-Ruel. Suzanne Valadon is the model for this painting, and her elegant figure is captured with effortless grace. The light touches her dress in a manner which only Renoir was able to achieve.

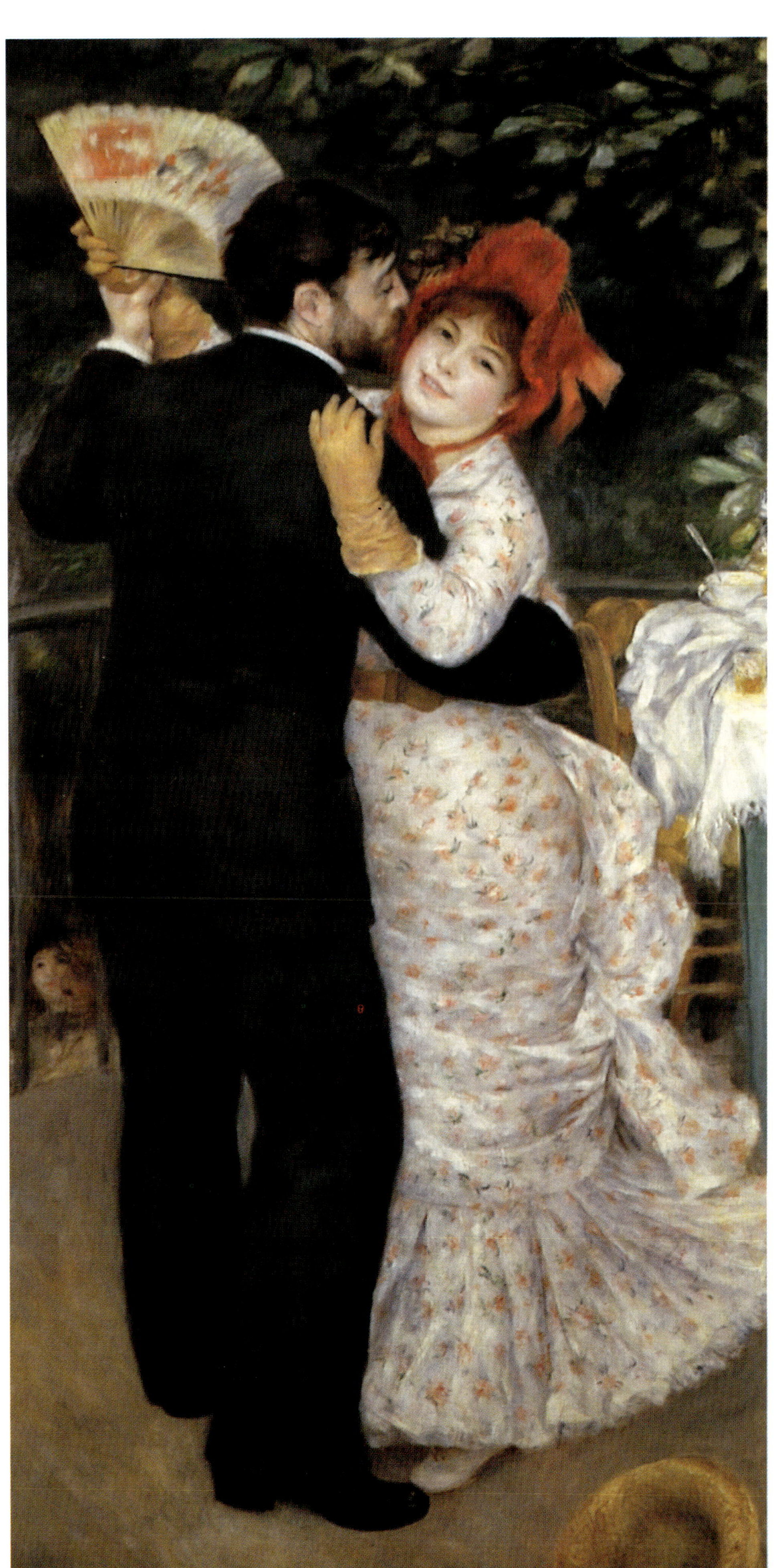

Dance in the Country, 1882-3 (Musée d'Orsay, Paris). The partner of *Dance in the City*, this painting has a more rustic and natural feel to it. Aline, Renoir's wife, is the model, and her generous figure contrasts greatly with that of Suzanne Valadon, the model of the former painting. It has been suggested that the contrast between the slim elegance of the city and the robustness of the country was intended.

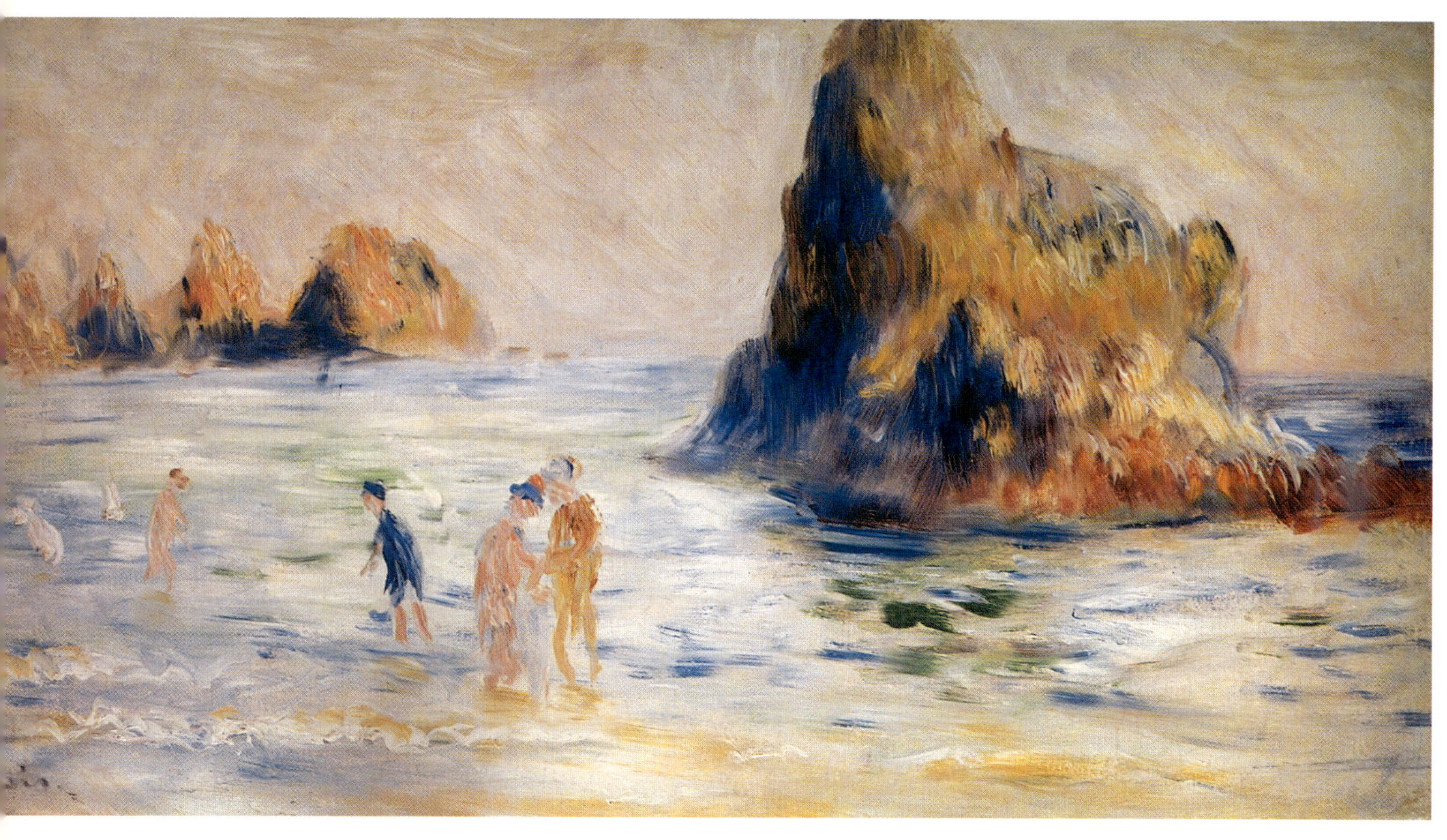

Guernsey, Moulin Huet Bay, 1883 (National Gallery, London). Renoir travelled a great deal throughout his career. In 1883 he made a trip with Monet along the Mediterranean and Monet's influence is evident in this painting. The colours are essentially Monet, and the composition is fairly conventional.

Opposite:
Seated Bather, *c.* 1892 (Private collection). One of many 'Seated Bathers' this painting is traditionally rendered, the sitter looking modestly away from the eyes of the viewer. Her skin is lustrous; her youth evident.

with more restrained colour. The emphasis shifted to accurate modelling, graphic precision, composition and extraordinary detail that detracts from the paintings as a whole, creating a confusion of aims that often drained the life from his subjects. By imposing a classical line on his characteristically cluttered paintings Renoir often deprived them of their soul, and the very essence of his work was forced to change.

When Renoir completed *The Umbrellas* in 1885, it was his final documentation of gay Parisian scenes; from this point on he sought to paint that which he considered to be timeless: evocative women unfettered by clothing and unable to be placed in any specific time or place; children and landscapes became much more prominent in his *oeuvre*, and robust still-lifes were a firm addition to his work.

But for the first few years after his trip to Italy, his subject matter and style changed only a little. He continued to paint portraits, his livelihood, and he continued to work on the human form, still in social settings. His *Dance* series was the last of his strictly Impressionist work, and it reflects the change his style was beginning to undergo.

Art dealer Paul Durand-Ruel commissioned Renoir to paint three impressions of the same size, on the theme of dancing. Renoir used Aline as the model for the first. A new Renoir model, Suzanne Valadon, is the subject of *Dance at Bougival* and *Dance in the City*. Suzanne was a painter in her own right, but she appeared often in

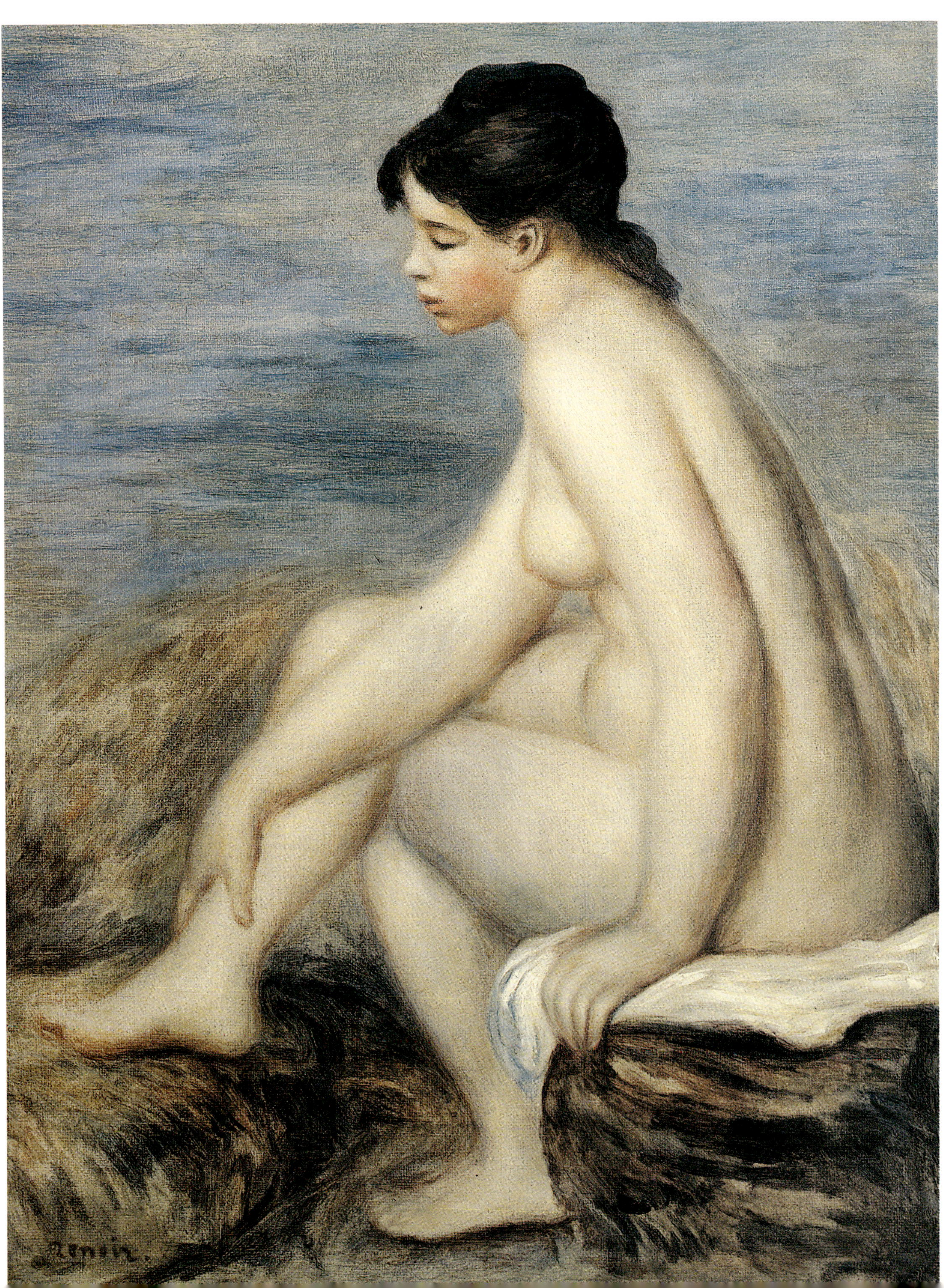
Renoir.

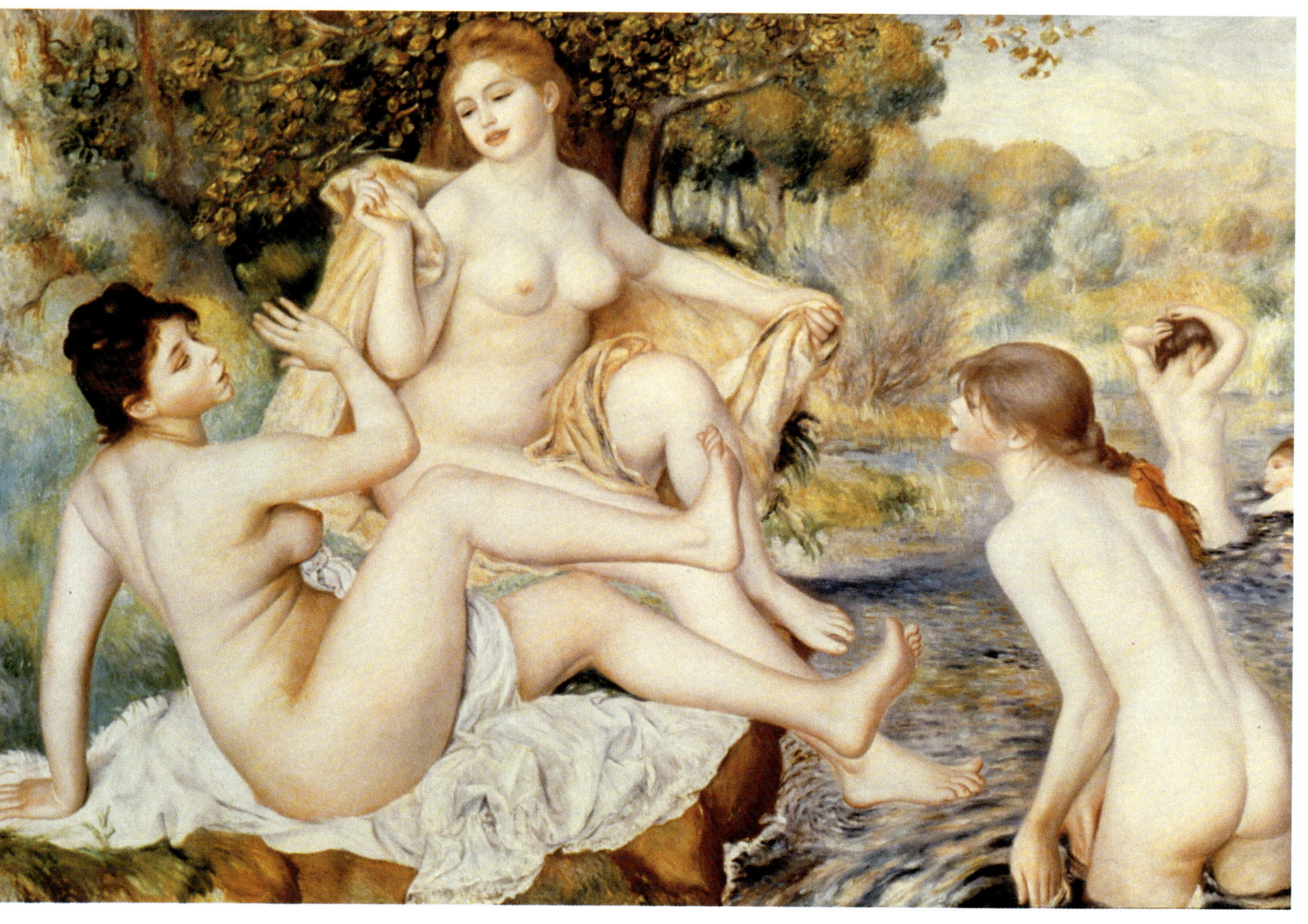

Bathers, 1887 (Philadelphia Museum of Art). This painting marked the culmination of Renoir's dry period. He has come a long way from the early days of his Impressionist technique. The bathers are no longer integrated with their background; indeed, their contours are delineated and explored. The painting was not painted out of doors, but in the studio, and the freshness of natural light that characterized so much of Renoir's work is not evident here.

Renoir's work. Unmarried, she gave birth to a son in 1883, whom some assumed to be fathered by Renoir himself.

Dance in the Country, the first in the series, is a typically cheerful painting, but is emblematic of Renoir's growing classical style. *Dance in the City,* the second, is more refined, losing only a little of the slightly cruder, perhaps more atmospheric feel of the first. Renoir's ability to recreate the fervour and energy of the dance is brilliantly displayed in the first two paintings, but by the third his couple has become stiff and far less lifelike. Renoir struggled with his new sensibility, and as a result many of his paintings lack the energy and wholesomeness of his earlier work.

Renoir's artistic crisis was no mystery; he sensed a problem and he spent the next years rectifying it. He said:

> *About 1883 I had wrung Impressionism dry, and I finally came to the conclusion that I knew neither how to paint nor how to draw. In a word, Impressionism was a blind alley, as far as I was concerned ...*

He no longer depended on Impressionist technique, and ceased to paint exclusively from nature. Instead he developed a system which depended on a large series of sketches and preparatory studies for each work, one which harked back to traditional schools of art and indeed his early days at Ecole des Beaux Arts. He expressed his new disenchantment with painting out of doors, where his preoccupation with form made it impossible to work at any speed. He said:

> *There is more density of light in the open air than in the studio where it remains unchangeable, whatever your intention or purpose may be. But this is precisely the reason why light is too important in the open air. There is no time to work out a compromise, and you can't see what you are doing.*

But Renoir's frustration was almost tangible. He struggled with form and the delineation of his subjects; he sought to teach himself the basics of art which had until that point been lacking in his education. However, by removing the spontaneity, he lost much of the character of his work and he tried continually to recapture that. Always a prolific artist, Renoir began to turn out far fewer finished paintings, resorting to selling his sketches to keep up a steady income. He wrote to Durand-Ruel from Italy in 1881, 'I am still suffering from experimenting. I'm not content and I am scraping off, still scraping off. I hope this craze will have an end ... I am still at the blotting stage and I am forty.'

Renoir did not exhibit in his dry period, a terrifying position for

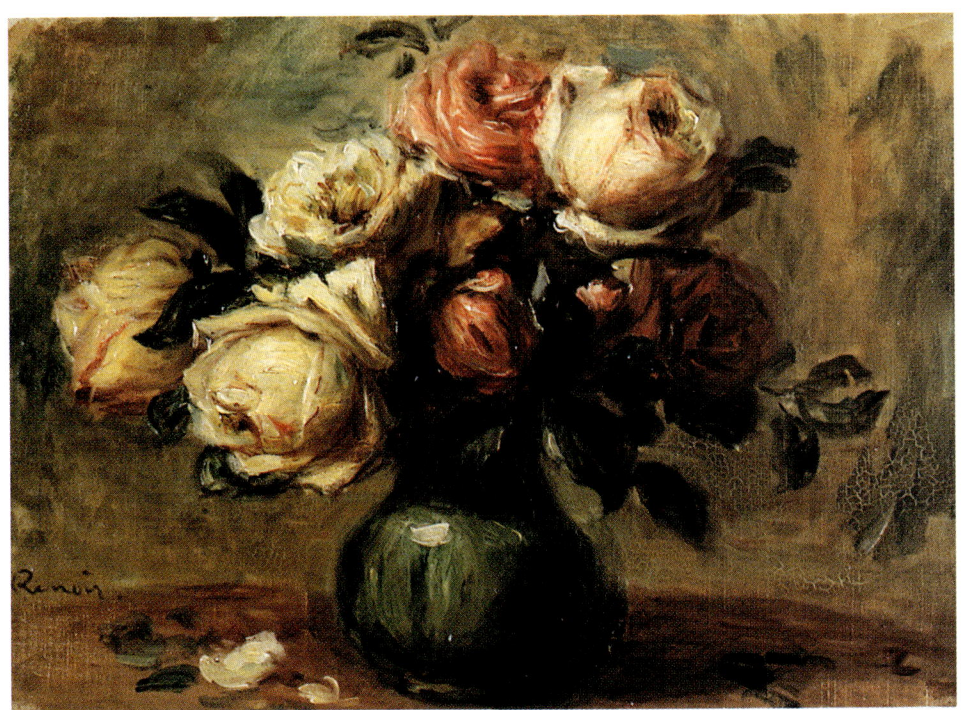

Still-life with Roses, 1890 (Cleveland Museum of Art). Renoir loved to paint roses, incorporating them into a number of his works. Earlier in his career he had painted dozens of ambitious and skilled still-lifes, which were much more eagerly sought than most of his other work. This painting is much simpler; the subject is the centre of the construction and there is no artifice. A petal has slipped from a blossom, a symbol of imperfection championed by Renoir.

an artist who depended on regular commissions and critical interest for his livelihood.

But Renoir had adopted a new sensibility. He emphasized his humility, saying that he was not an artist but a painter, a kind of tradesman in the tradition of his father and all the other craftsmen whose livelihoods had been threatened by the industrial age. John House, in 'Renoir's Worlds' points out:

> *In his descriptions of his own art he emphasized the prime importance of artisanal experience, values which echoed his father's trade and his own first training ... He always distanced himself from the theorists and intellectuals of painting; but occasionally he also felt the need to emphasize that his modest claims for his art should not be taken to literally, and that painting was something more than mere craftsmanship: a true painter needed 'finesse and charm' and also 'serenity'; his work should give evidence of the 'supremacy of mind'.*

There is some evidence that the plethora of Renoir sketches on the market damaged his reputation. In 1903 Durand-Ruel wrote to Renoir, saying, 'You have been quite wrong to give away or allow people to take from you all these rough sketches which people are now circulating everywhere in order to prevent the sale of your fine paintings.' But Renoir was compelled to paint, and because of the frustration he felt throughout this period, he was unable to complete whole paintings in the manner to which he was previously accustomed, filling canvases with dozens of tiny sketches instead. His compulsion to work has been compared to a nervous tic, a manifestation of his innate restlessness.

But to assume that all of the work that was produced during this period was bad would be misleading. While much of it differed enormously from his earlier carefree style, Renoir's paintings still betrayed his genius. Artistic crisis or not, Renoir had an unsurpassed ability to achieve greatness on his canvas, bringing to life his subjects in a manner which in no way reflected the discontent he was experiencing. Aside from the *Dance* series, he continued with his portraiture and a number of landscapes.

He continued to paint the human form, but with much more refinement. The eighties marked a new interest in nudes, and he painted dozens. One of his greatest masterpieces, painted in 1883-4 was *Seated Bather*, created in Guernsey and reflecting the development of his classical technique. The bather is distinct from her background for the first time; his subejct is contoured and much more classically rendered, and yet Renoir was able to retain the vigour and suggestiveness of an Impressionist background. Renoir's nudes have often been berated for their unrealistic aspect – all his women are comely,

Mme Renoir with Child, 1886 (Cleveland Museum of Art). Aline and Renoir's son Pierre were the subjects of many of his paintings. He delighted in the relationship between mother and son, and effortlessly portrayed them in repose or at any one of their day-to-day activities. In this painting the background has become more important, unusually for Renoir, playing a role in the story related by the work.

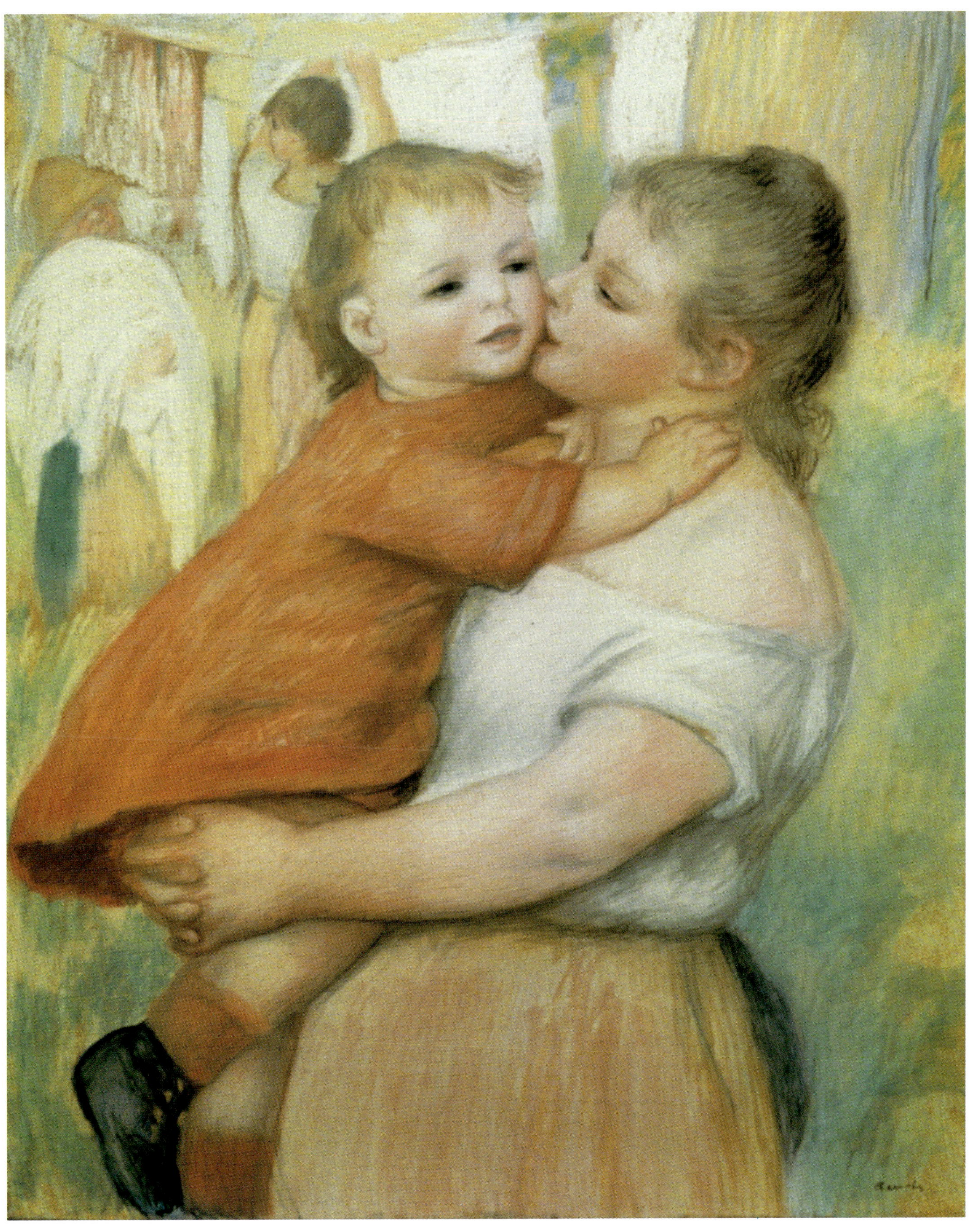

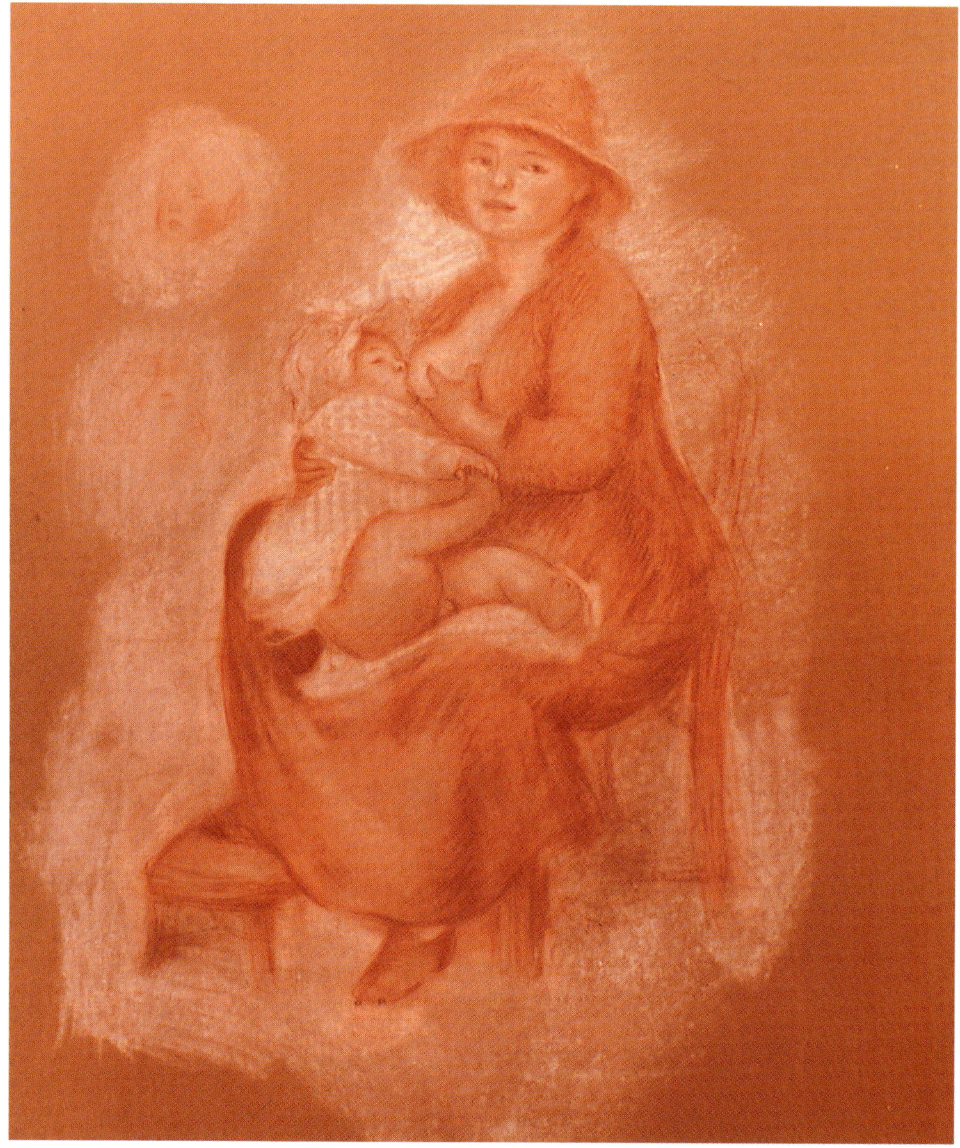

Maternity, 1886 (Museum of Fine Arts, St Petersburg, Florida). Aline and Renoir's first son Pierre are the subject of this moving and enormously sensual picture. The composition recalls a classical Madonna and Child, and since Renoir was currently suffering his first artistic crisis, it is likely that this is the precisely the quality he sought.

unabashed and inviting; curvaceous but never fat. Degas in particular riled his colleague for their fantastic nature, arguing that no woman really sat in the midst of nature, brushing her hair or bathing. But Renoir had had some experience of immodest bathing in Guernsey. In the autumn of 1883 he wrote to Durand-Ruel:

> *One would think oneself in a Watteau landscape rather than in reality ... Just as in Athens the women are not at all afraid of the proximity of men on the nearby rocks. Nothing is more amusing, while one is strolling through these rocks, than surprising young girls getting ready to bathe; even though they are English they are not particularly shocked.*

Renoir travelled a great deal throughout his period of discontent, often bringing Aline with him for parts of his journeys. The point at which he made a firm commitment to Aline is unknown, but he did not move in with her until 1895, after the birth of their first son, and he did not marry her for another five years. They lived in rented accommodation, first in his studio in the rue Saint-Georges, and then, soon after their marriage in 1890, in the 'Chateau des Brouillards' in rue Girardon. He continued to make Paris his base, creating for himself and Aline a simple existence. His son Jean later described their life on rue Girardon:

> *The inhabitants, enclosed within the high hedge and enjoying a certain privacy behind the fences of their own small gardens, dwelt in a world apart, concealing endless fantasy under a provincial exterior.*

He continued:

> *All along our fence there were rose-bushes which had reverted to their wild state. Just beyond was an orchard belonging to old Gries, one of the last market-gardeners on the heights of Montmartre. For most Parisians this little paradise of lilacs and roses seemed like the end of the world.*

From this rural haven which he had created among the hubbub of Paris, he continued the travels that would quell his wanderlust, allowing him to enjoy more fully some form of family life, and create the opportunity for experimentation in this time of crisis.

He worked with Cézanne in L'Estaque in France, and travelled with Monet along the Mediterranean coast. He visited too Aline Charigot's native village of Essoyes, but he remained restless, wallowing not in the opportunities for splendid landscapes that these voyages afforded him, but seeking instead 'the perfect model'. He told Monet ruefully that he was a figure painter, and could not rest until he was able to do justice to the timeless beauty of the human form. His continued to paint landscapes, documenting his travels across his own country, into Algiers and Italy, and across to the Channel Islands. But some of the most splendid of his works were painted not from nature but from sketches, and from memory.

Probably the most representative work of this period is *The Bathers*, inspired by Girardon's *Bain de Diane*. The landscape and the figures were obviously painted indoors, and Cézanne's influence is evident in the composition. He moves away in this painting from the Impressionist ideal of capturing an instant in a painting, towards a more ageless vision of woman within nature.

He experimented with both outline, now either firmly inked on the canvas before he began work, or carefully brushed in afterwards, and with his methods of painting. He had become discontent with oil painting and he investigated a variety of techniques, including the avoidance of oil almost entirely. This created the appearance of enamel - or as one critic suggested, porcelain, which recalled his first trade. But without oil, his paintings were not properly preserved, and they began to disintegrate.

The Bathers implemented many of these new techniques, but Renoir was obviously not confident of their impact for he gave the painting a subtitle for the show at Georges Petit's Expositions internationales in 1886, calling it *Trial for Decorative Painting*. Around this time Renoir also prepared a proposal for the creation of a society to celebrate irregularity in art, which he felt had been obliterated by the age of mass-production. He published a 'Summary of the Grammar of the Arts', which focused on the loss of craftsmanship over the previous decades. He blamed the current lack of original art on this loss, and formed a premise which explained that integral beauty was only possible in irregularity. Sadly, nothing was to come of his ideas, but they clearly illustrate the dissatisfaction Renoir was experiencing, and his inability to find some kind of solace.

The Bathers was greeted with horror by a large number of Renoir's patrons and friends, many of whom mourned the loss of his dependably cheerful and agreeably untidy style. The painting was considered artificial, which the Impressionists categorically railed against. He did, however, receive some encouragement. Berthe Morisot thought that 'one cannot go further in the rendering of form', and Monet, as he often did, seemed to understand the direction in which Renoir was moving. His requests for portraits died out throughout this period of experimentation, and even Durand-Ruel, his champion, found it difficult to reconcile this new form of art, buying very few paintings during his *periode aigre*.

While the structure and nature of Renoir's work throughout this time dismayed many art lovers, it is certain that Renoir did continue to paint with the same fervour and emotion invested in his earlier work. The spontaneity of composition may have been extinguished under the new pressures he placed upon himself, but his paintings remained alive and vibrant.

He painted *Maternity* in this period, a timeless and evocative painting in which Aline nurses their young son Pierre. He has undertaken much of the classical influence - the figures are carefully outlined and delineated from the background, and the scene is evocative of a Renaissance Madonna and child. However, there is a freshness about the painting that betrays its calculated structure. Pierre's foot is caught in mid-air and his flesh is as sensuous as it is in any of Renoir's previous images. There is a warmth and friendliness about the painting; it is an intimate moment shared without false modesty. While

Head of a Young Girl, 1890 (Chicago Institute of Art). The lush and luminous flesh of this model demonstrates the new maturity of Renoir's vision of women. A casual, slightly messy hairstyle is the ultimate contrast to the creamy perfection of the skin.

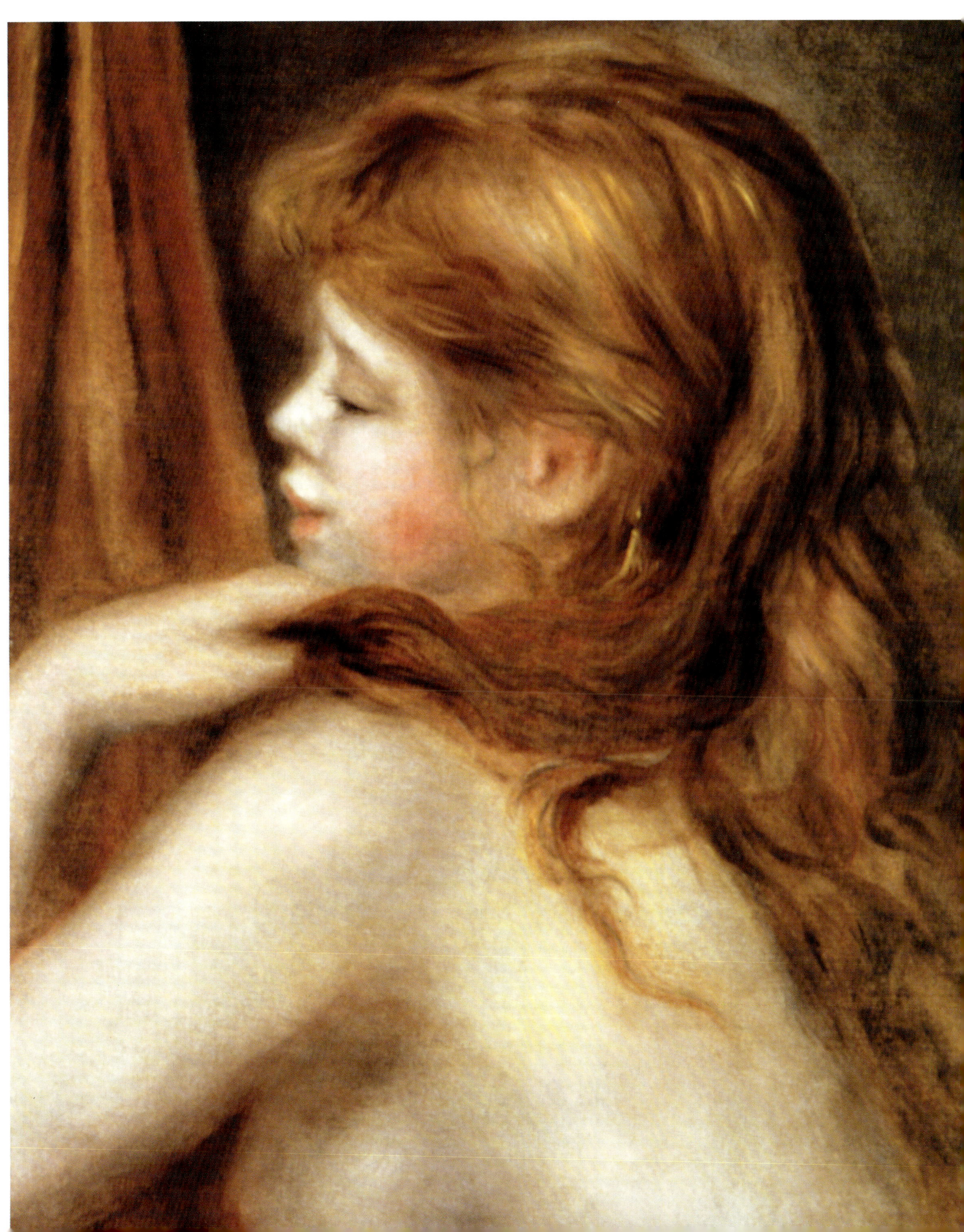

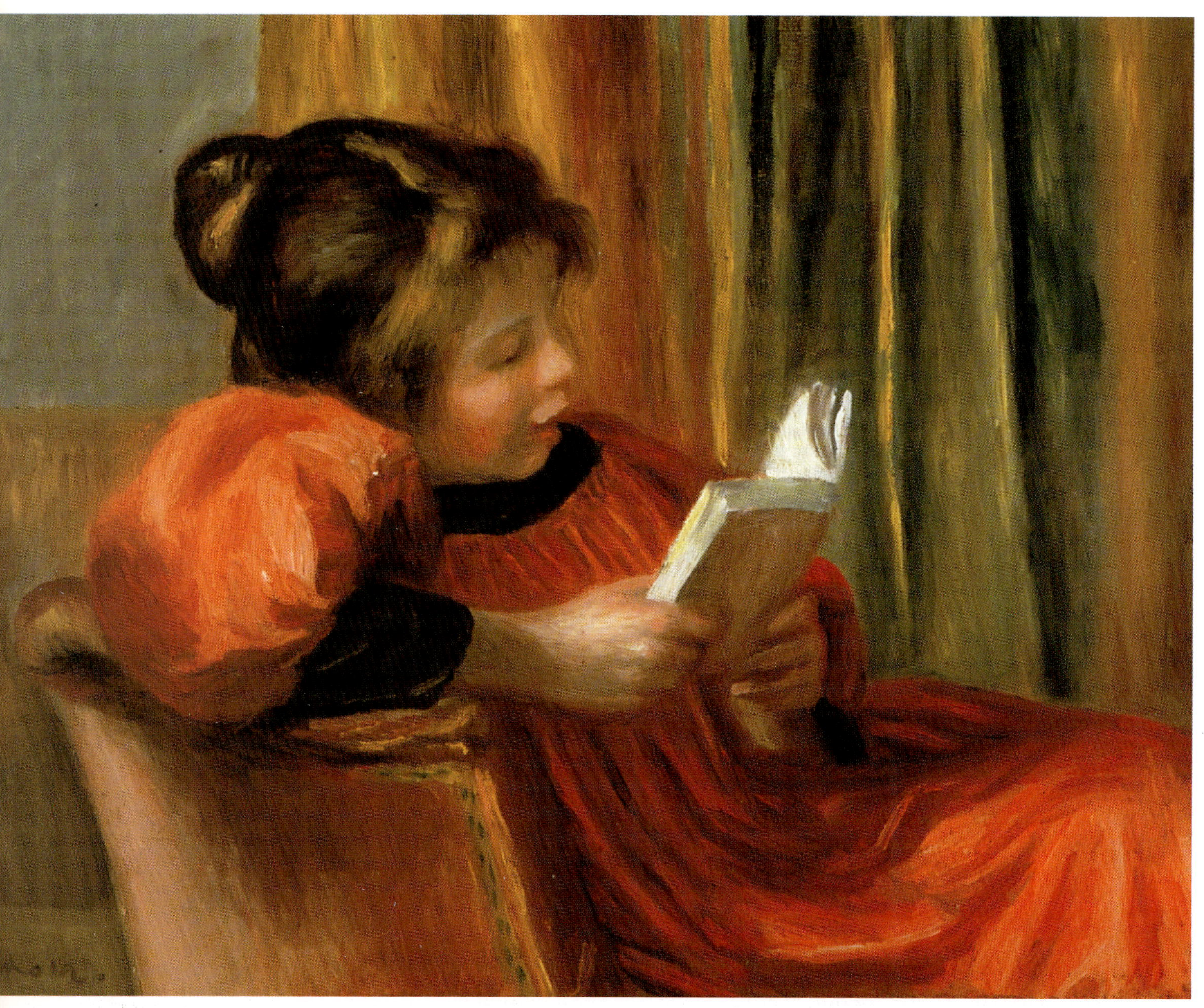

Girl Reading, 1890 (Houston Museum of Fine Arts). The richer colours and firmer contouring of his post-dry period work are evident in this painting. Women at leisure was a popular theme throughout Renoir's *oeuvre*, and this charming portrait captures effortlessly the luminescence of the sitter's skin, and the casual manner with which she holds her book.

Renoir may have changed the manner in which he portrayed his subjects, he still managed to evoke their very essence.

Maternity like *The Bathers*, was the culmination of Renoir's dry period, which would move forward into a style that celebrated the human form, creating in it a luminescence that would come to represent Renoir's more mature style. From 1888 Renoir's second crisis resulted in the 'Pearly Period'. He systematically destroyed much of his previous work, looking for a new depth and sensuousness in half-tones of pink and white. His linear style was phased out eventually and he entered into the style that would remain with him for the rest of his working life. Critics of his work were converted by the magnificence of his women – exquisite textures, sumptuous expanses of flesh and splendidly uncontrived scenes rewarded Renoir with a new following. He had at great length come to terms with his own style, choosing now to enliven it rather than experiment any further. He explained this new technique with some humility:

> *I arrange my subject as I want it, then I go ahead and paint it, like a child. I want a red to be sonorous, to sound like a bell; if it doesn't turn out that way, I put more reds or other colours till I get it. I am no cleverer than that. I have no rules and no methods; any one can look at my materials or watch how I paint – he will see that I have no secrets. I look at a nude; there are myriad of tiny tints. I must find the ones that will make the flesh on my canvas live and quiver.*

In actual fact, Renoir worked with a very limited palette, perhaps some eight to ten colours, but his skill at implementing them to create such languorous, supremely tactile women is unprecedented and, indeed, unmatched today. It has been suggested that Renoir loved women to such an extent that a deep understanding of them evolved in him, allowing this extraordinary insight to shine through in his work. Men and women delight in his nudes – there is nothing lewd or voyeuristic, nor is there anything contrived. Renoir allowed the Impressionist spontaneity to attach itself to his timeless and elegant compositions, giving them a freshness that was missing from most work with the human form. He said to his son Jean:

> *I love women. They doubt nothing. With them the world becomes something very simple. They give everything its correct value and well realize that their laundry is as important as the constitution of the German empire. Near them one feels reassured.*

John House, in 'Renoir's Worlds', points out that it was by his representation of women that Renoir wanted his powers as a painter to be assessed. He notes, 'In the early 1890s he commented that "in literature as well as in painting, talent is shown only by the treatment of the feminine figures". The art of a Degas or a Manet gives lie to this as a generalization; but Renoir certainly revealed himself most fully in the image of women that he constructed in his paintings – both his sensory sybaritism and his fear of overt emotional or intellectual engagement.'

His relationship with Aline was complex. She represented for him a kind of earthy peasantry that salved a soul rent by nostalgia and longing for the society of yesteryear. She was quite like his mother, a strong and stolid woman who asked little of life and gave a great deal. She dealt with the frivolities of life, laying their table with good, plain food and organizing Renoir's affairs so that he was free to paint, to travel and to socialize with a set in which she never felt comfortable, but which, surprisingly, she did not challenge or long for. It is doubtful whether her company was anything more than a deep comfort and source of affection for her husband; he wrote to his friend Gallimard in 1900, 'I am fine, but I need a man. It's rather boring in the evening.'

But Renoir's talents have never been so fully realized as when he painted women. His lush, buxom ladies, many of whom shared the same face and physique, were exquisitely rendered; Renoir's women held an allure that many painters would spend their careers attempting to capture. After the birth of his son he began to paint children in the same naturalistic manner, portraying them in their childish games, at a meal with their nurse, breastfeeding, asleep on an arm, at the piano or reading a book. The innocence and unfettered charm of his paintings avoided any kind of manipulated sentimentality. No one else could portray so clearly the carefree days of childhood, the joy of living on a sunlit afternoon. Renoir painted children as he saw them and while there would always be a margin of fantasy in his work, he never attempted to force his audience to feel anything.

Although his personal life had settled, and he resolved the crises in his art, Renoir continued to live the life of a nomad, travelling throughout the 1890s in France, Holland and Spain, and moving his own home from Montmartre to three other addresses in Paris before he finally bought a house in Essoyes in Burgundy, the home village of Aline. And then there was Cagnes, where Renoir and his family moved in 1903, and this marked the final change in his work. There was a new maturity, a comprehension that had never before existed in his work. Renoir had grown up.

Gabrielle and Jean, 1900 (Musée de l'Orangerie, Paris). The birth of Renoir's son Jean brought Gabrielle, a nursemaid who became one of Renoir's favourite models, into their home. She is the subject of countless works, often with the Renoir children, who were allowed to play happily while they were being painted. Renoir sought to capture the integral charm of an unwatched moment.

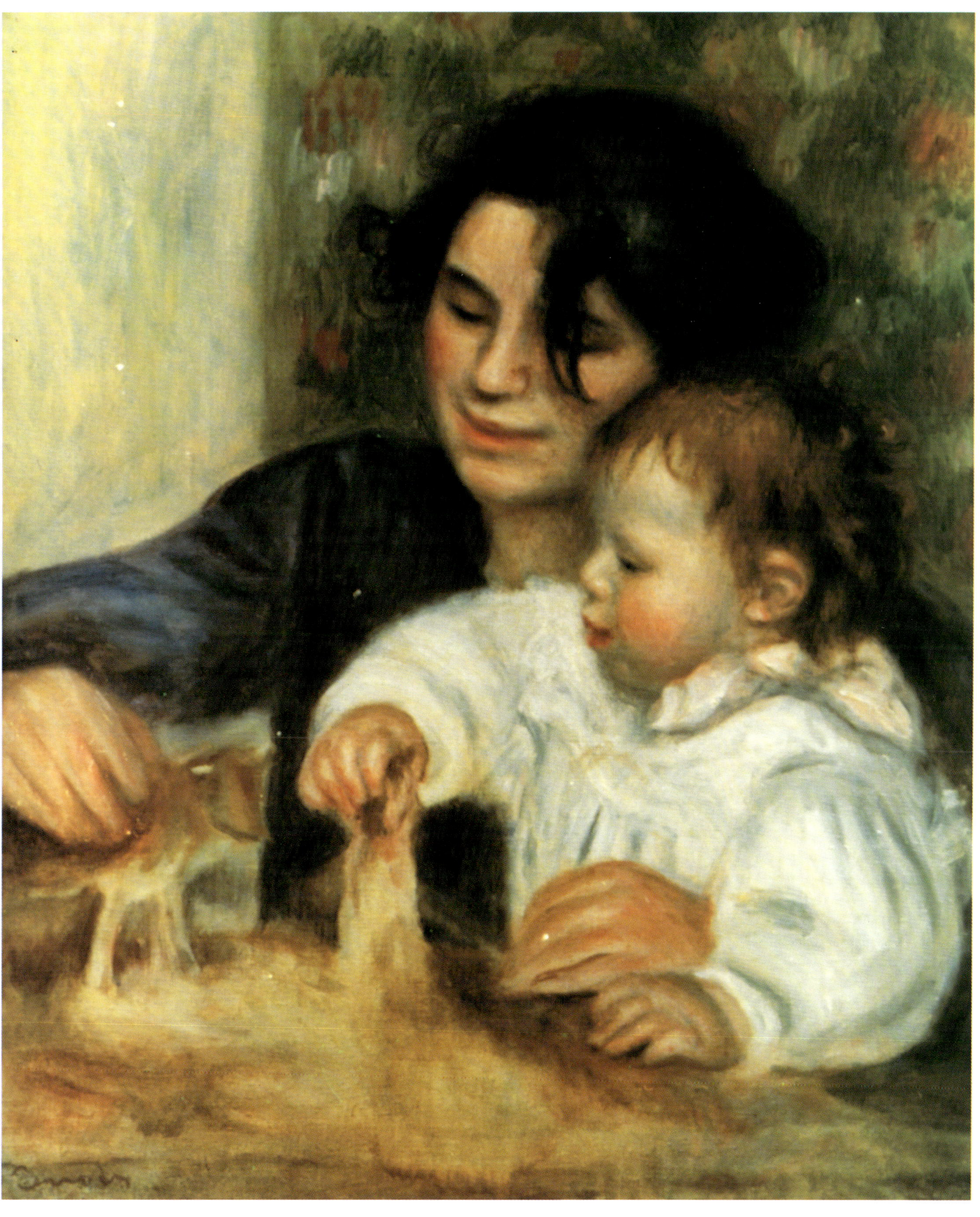

CHAPTER 4

The Mature Years

By the end of the eighties Renoir was beginning to savour the success of a mature and now acclaimed artist. He was content with his art, with his family. He was beginning to put down roots that were for him symbols of a growing satisfaction.

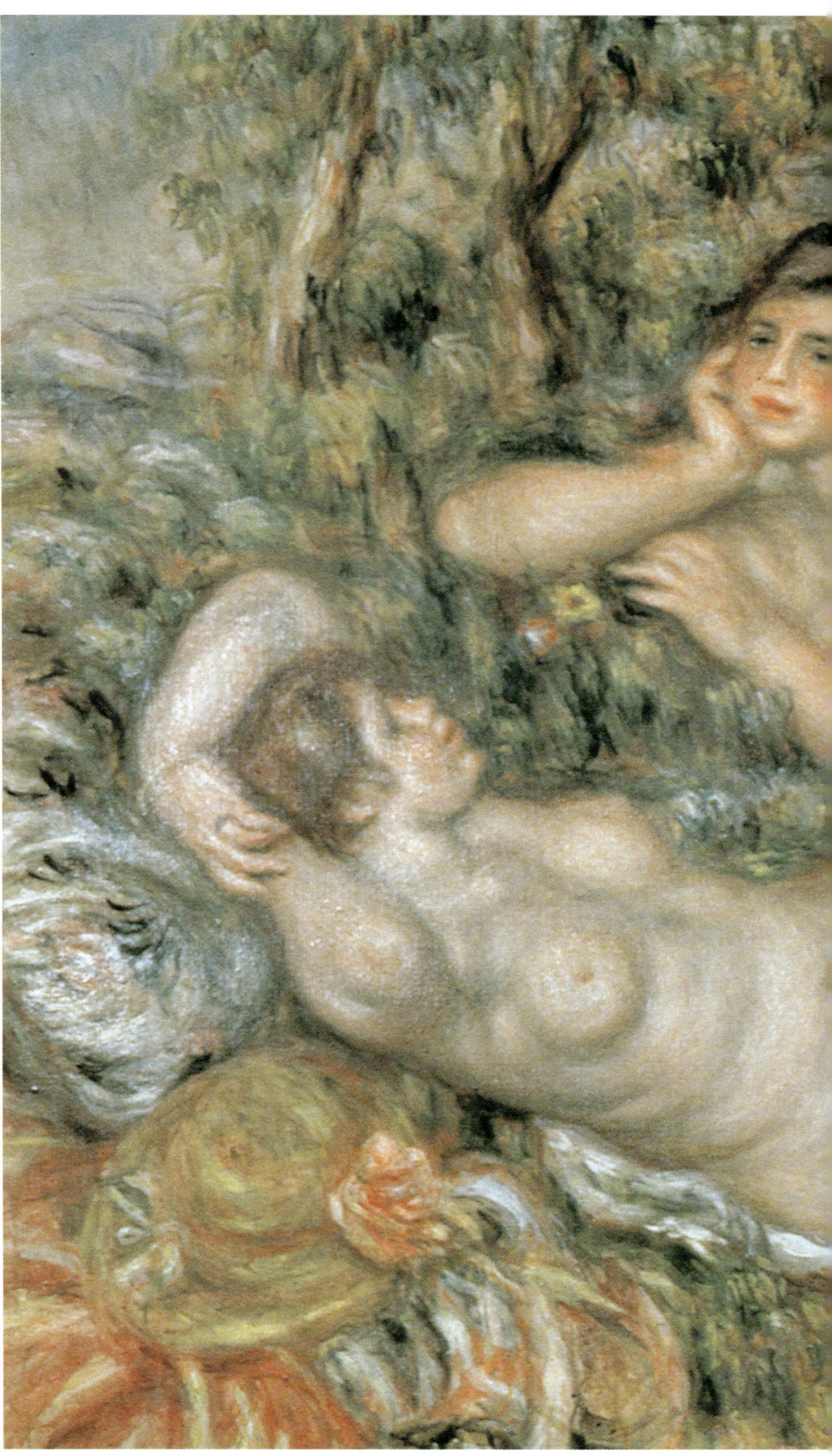

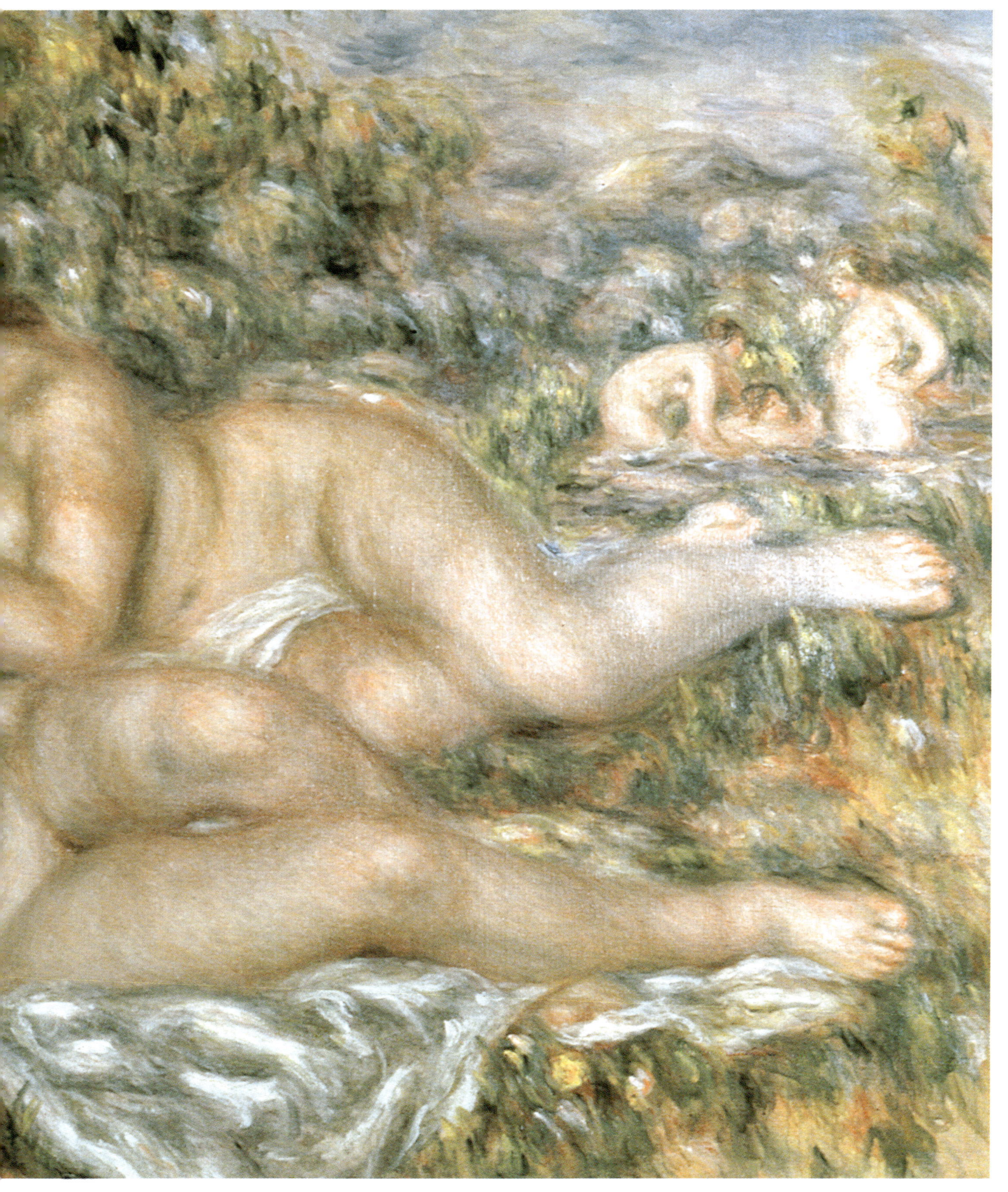

Overleaf:
Bathers, c. 1918-19 (Musée d'Orsay, Paris). Renoir's last finished masterpiece, this painting is a remarkable tribute to the painter's mature techniques. There was and still is some feminist outcry about the nature of the women he painted; the delight evident in the strong, confident brushstrokes makes this not a satire, or an exercise in voyeurism, but a strong and sensual celebration of the female form, which he had painted unceasingly throughout his career.

Opposite:
Monsieur Germain, 1900 (Norton Museum of Art, Palm Beach, Florida). By the early 1900s, Renoir had become a popular portraitist. The cheerful splashes of colour that characterized his earlier work had been replaced with a more sombre and composed style, but he retained his gift for revealing the personality of the sitter.

It is ironic that illness struck Renoir at such a happy time in his life, bringing with it a long and painful affliction that would make increasingly difficult the very things that had made his life worthwhile.

His first attack of rheumatism came in 1888, following a chill; rheumatoid arthritis came shortly thereafter and the progress of the disease was uncompromising. For the next decade he became physically emaciated, his hands losing their shape and control. By the turn of the century he walked only with the aid of a walking stick and to his horror he was wheelchair-bound just under a decade later. But Renoir's work remained largely unaffected by this unsightly and extremely painful condition. Due in part perhaps to his training as a porcelain painter, and to the rigorous retraining he gave himself in the eighties, his work retained its fluency and delicacy. He was able to exhibit remarkable agility despite the fact that he was often unable to hold a paintbrush.

But Renoir took a new and even greater pleasure in painting the simple things in life and while his illness denied him the travels he had enjoyed and indeed needed so thoroughly, it did allow him to savour the warmth of his family, and the everyday events that would become the new subjects for his work. His family had extended over the years to include two other sons, Jean in 1894 and Claude, nicknamed Coco, in 1901. A series of nursemaids looked after the children, and also played the role of model. Gabrielle Renard, in particular, remained with the family for nearly twenty years, appearing in countless of Renoir's most exquisitely rendered works. After Gabrielle, a local girl called Marie Dupuis took over, working happily at housework until she was summoned by her master. Renoir's children were the subjects of many of his works, but they were not forced to pose or to take up an occupation which might bore them. Instead he painted them at play, at rest or at whatever activity had caught their attention. He relished their freedom and worked to capture its essence. John House explains:

> *... he was fascinated by childhood, seeking to recreate in his paintings of children his idea of the child's immediate response to visual experience, unconditioned by the knowledge of good and evil; he was enchanted by children, he told Roux-Champion, because 'their mouths utter only the words which animals would utter if they could talk.'*

By this end of Renoir's artistic crisis, much of his time was spent away from Paris. Renoir had finally found some satisfaction with his art and he no longer needed to seek the reassurance and inspiration of his contemporaries, or the great works in the museums, which he had continued to call upon throughout his career to advise its direction.

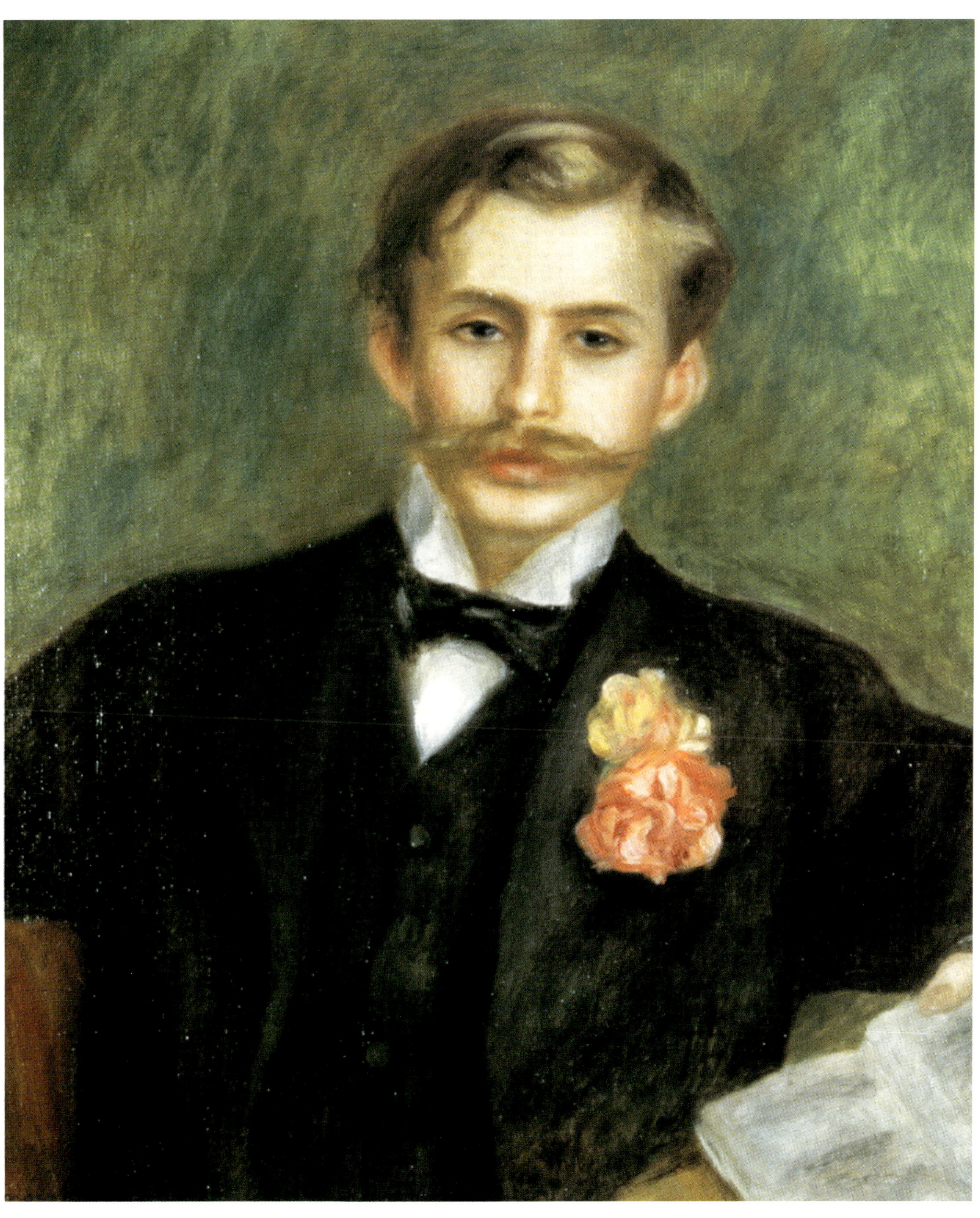

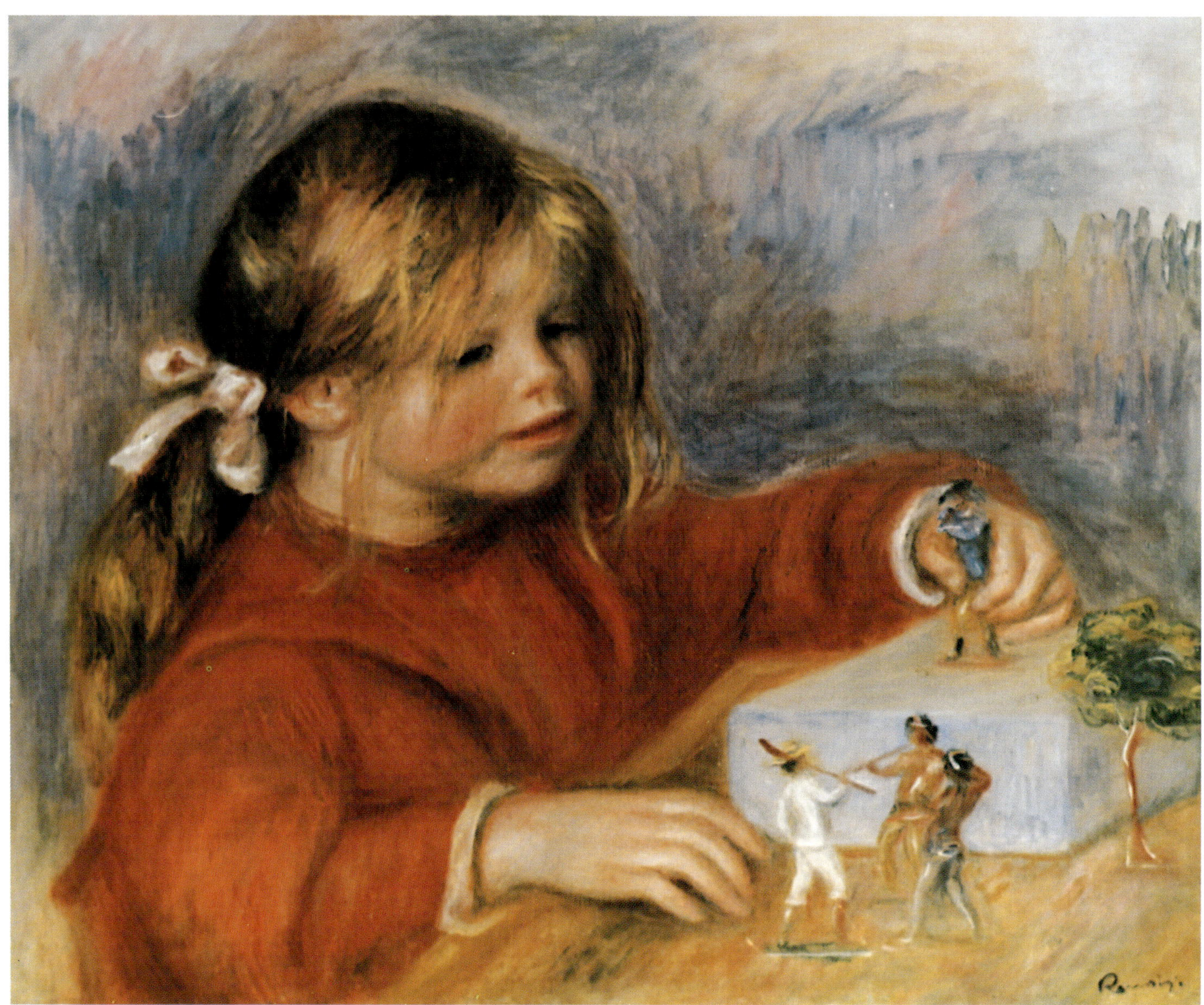

Claude Renoir Playing, 1905 (Musée de l'Orangerie, Paris). Renoir liked nothing better than to document his children at play. He had an amazing ability to seize an instant in his children's lives, catching an innocent expression here, a moment of solitude there, and creating an exquisite portrait of childhood that was neither over-sentimental nor contrived.

They had begun to spend summers at their house near Essoyes, and in 1903 they went to Cagnes sur Mer, just west of Nice, where they eventually bought land and built a house in 1907.

Renoir continued to see his group of Parisian friends. His relationship with Monet continued until his death, and he always had a great compassion for the other artist's work. So too did he praise Cézanne, whose work he understood – perhaps because of the time they spent painting together. Sisley and his wife too remained good friends, as did Morisot, Manet and his Paris set of dealers, but Renoir spent less time seeking out their views, and since many were reaching old age, and becoming less mobile, they often kept in touch by letter instead.

The move to the South of France was prompted by Renoir's illness, but permitted by his now sanguine attitude to his own work. He had become much more complaisant, and he revelled in the countryside that had become his home. He wrote, 'In this marvellous country, it seems as if misfortune cannot befall one; one is cosseted by the atmosphere.'

But Renoir's inherent restlessness did surface here and there. He resented greatly the commercialization of the south of France and as he had throughout his career, he battled against the landmarks of progress. There are several interesting and amusing stories about the mass of contradictions that comprised his character. The first incident concerned his love of activity and noise, which he loved to surround him. He was a notorious hummer, filling any silences with snippets of song. He loved conversation and music and laughter. But when his son Jean was given a phonograph he reacted violently against the intrusion in his home, noting that it threatened to destroy a 'great blessing: silence'.

He immediately left the first home they were renting in Cagnes when the orange grove across the street was uprooted for a new development, and he eventually bought Les Collettes, the home at which they remained for most of the remainder of his life, because its olive groves were threatened. Aline convinced him to build a massive stone farmhouse on the land, but he refused to paint it – enjoying its spectacular views, but despising its newness.

He cultivated a kind of unkempt appearance, wanting neither a garden or a villa, but an overgrown estate in which nature was allowed to run its course. He wanted his home to reflect what once took place there – a celebration of the old, again characteristic of Renoir's nostalgia.

His paintings of women began to take on a more comfortable, mature aspect, and he rejected the fashionable society of his earlier work for the simple pleasures of his own garden, his studio and the landscape that surrounded him. His illness prevented him from producing large-scale works, but smaller paintings were rigorously turned out, and sketches from that period abound. In the early years of the twentieth century, Renoir adopted a palette that was cool and spartan; later, red became a predominant colour and he used paint in a much more lavish manner, retaining at once the fluency of his earlier technique and endowing it with a sort of gay abandon.

He painted still-lifes as well, bowls of flowers, the remnants of a meal – nothing frivolous or artificial. He said once:

> *What seems to me to be one of the most important things about our movement is that we have freed painting from the tyranny of subject-matter. I am free to paint flowers and call them flowers, without having to weave a story around them.*

In fact he painted more and more flowers in his later years, finding comfort in their individuality. He told Georges Rivière later:

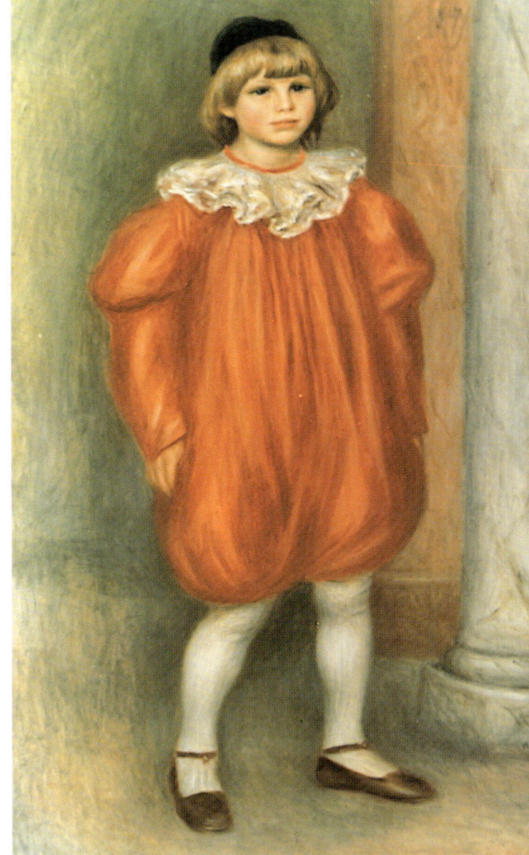

The Clown, 1909 (Musée de l'Orangerie, Paris). Renoir's youngest son, Claude (Coco), is the subject of the painting. Dressed in a clown costume, Coco is given the treatment of a court portrait. Despite the magnitude of the work, Renoir kept it for himself until his death.

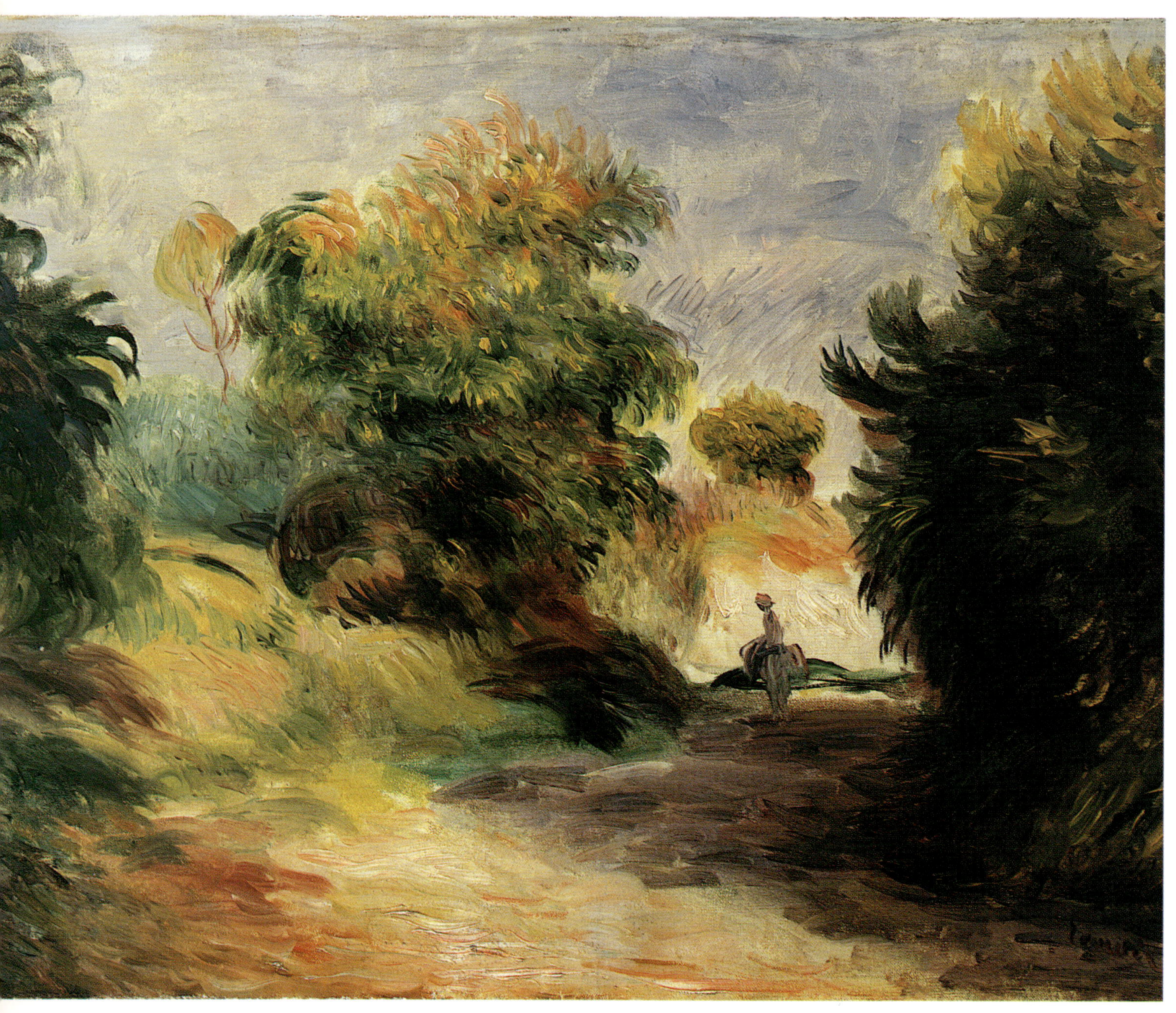

Countryside near Cagnes, 1907 (Private collection). Abundantly stormier than Renoir's Impressionist landscapes, this painting reflects the warmth of his more mature palette. Many critics derided this later work.

Painting flowers is a form of mental relaxation. I do not need the concentration that I need when I am faced with a model. When I am painting flowers I can experiment boldly with tones and values without worrying about destroying the whole painting. I would not dare to do that with a figure because I would be afraid of spoiling everything. The experience I gain from these experiments can then be applied to my paintings.

Towards the end of the 1890s, Renoir had advised Julie Manet to take up still-life painting in order to teach herself to paint quickly. It is evident that Renoir did paint the hundreds of still-lifes that exist very

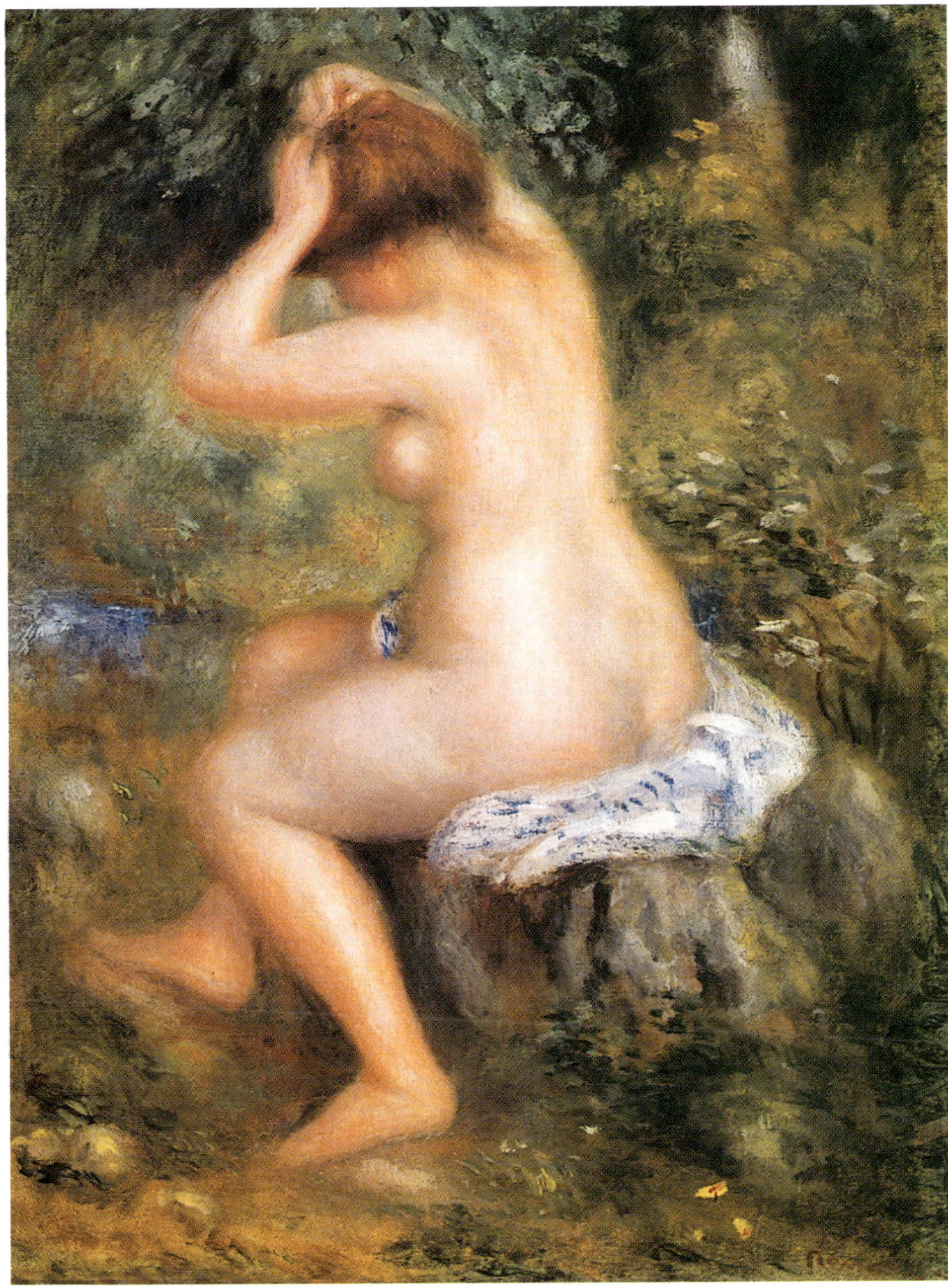

Nude, *c.* 1885-90 (National Gallery, London). Renoir's nudes, or 'bathers' as they were most often labelled, were usually at some stage of an intimate toilet. Degas argued that Renoir's nudes were unrealistic, that women simply didn't sit in gardens without a scrap of clothing, dressing their hair.

quickly, filling any creative gaps that occurred, and taking a break from the strains of figure painting when suffering from bouts of arthritis. Paul Durand-Ruel objected to the number of Renoir sketches and half-finished works flooding the market, to which Renoir replied, 'if I only sold good things, I would die of hunger'.

Renoir's work was, however, achieving the kind of recognition he had sought for most of his life. In 1892, the French government bought its first Renoir, a painting entitled *Young Girls at the Piano.* Renoir was distraught by this choice, feeling that another of his works might have been more suitable, that it was not an accurate reflection of his work. He worried needlessly; the painting was much admired and Renoir's

Portrait of Aline Charigot (Madame Renoir), 1885 (Philadelphia Museum of Art). One of the few existing portraits of Aline, this was painted just after the birth of their first son Pierre. She is portrayed here as a sturdy woman, in sensible almost peasant clothes, a contrast to the gay and fashionable impression of her in *Luncheon of the Boating Party*.

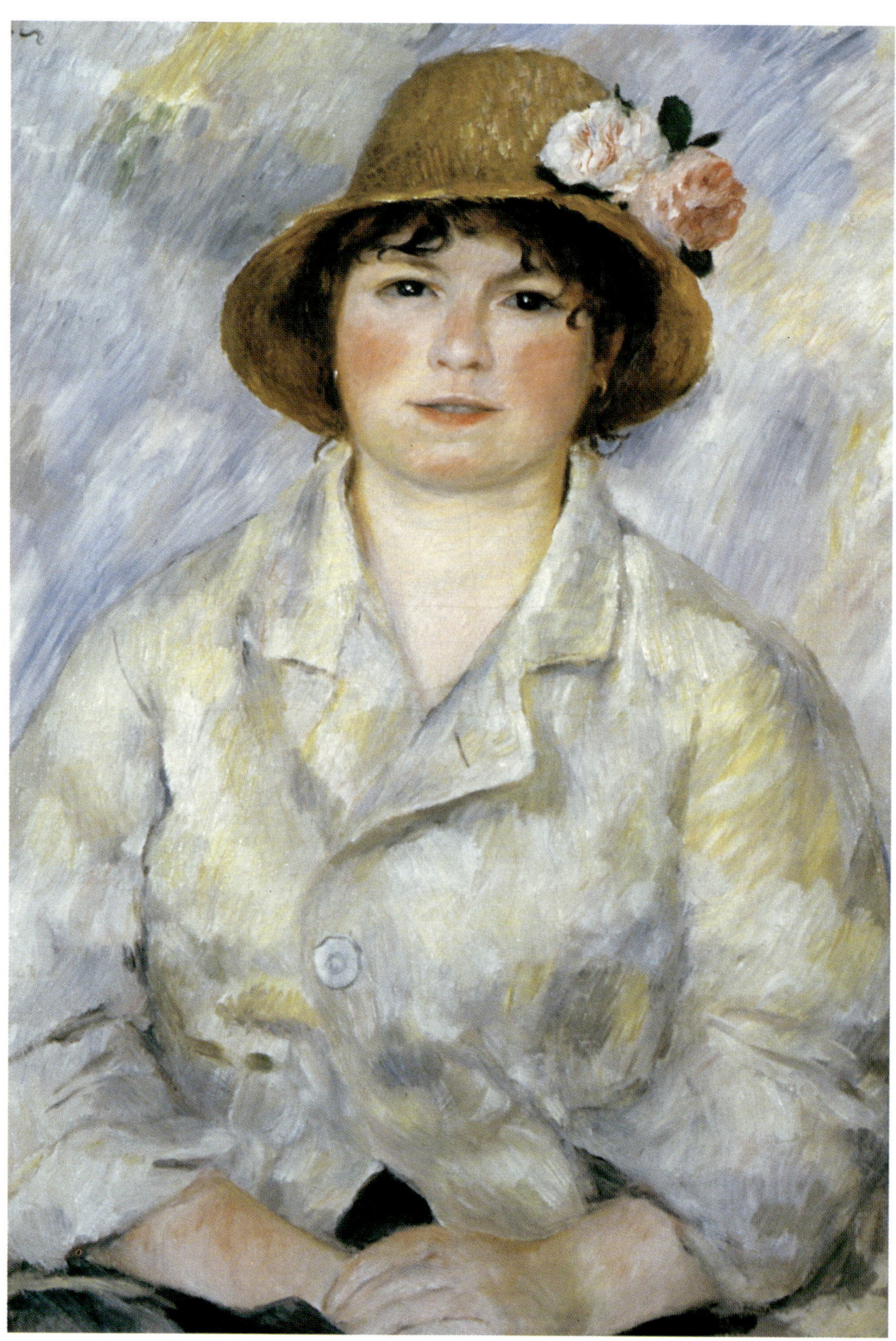

following subsequently grew, increasing the prices paid for his work and the number of commissions offered. His pride in his work was overwhelmingly humble. He wrote:

> *When I look at the old masters I feel a simple little man, yet I believe that among my works there will be enough to assure me a place in the French School, that school which I love so much, which is so pretty, so clear, such good company ...*

He continued to paint some portraits, but mainly his portrayals of the human form were limited to his children and to the various models he took on. The last years of his life were difficult ones. His two oldest sons were wounded in the war, the shock of which is said to have led directly to the illness and eventual death of Aline in 1915. Renoir was deeply affected by her death and he found himself increasingly isolated in a house that was empty of its central warmth, and trapped by an illness that threatened to immobilize him completely. He continued to paint, the one solace in his life, but suddenly it was no longer enough. It was during this period that he began to spend long periods of time with his son Jean, who would later write *Renoir, My Father*. Jean went on to become an acknowledged genius in the world of film, but during this time he fostered the relationship with his father, and he developed a deep and sensitive understanding of him and his work.

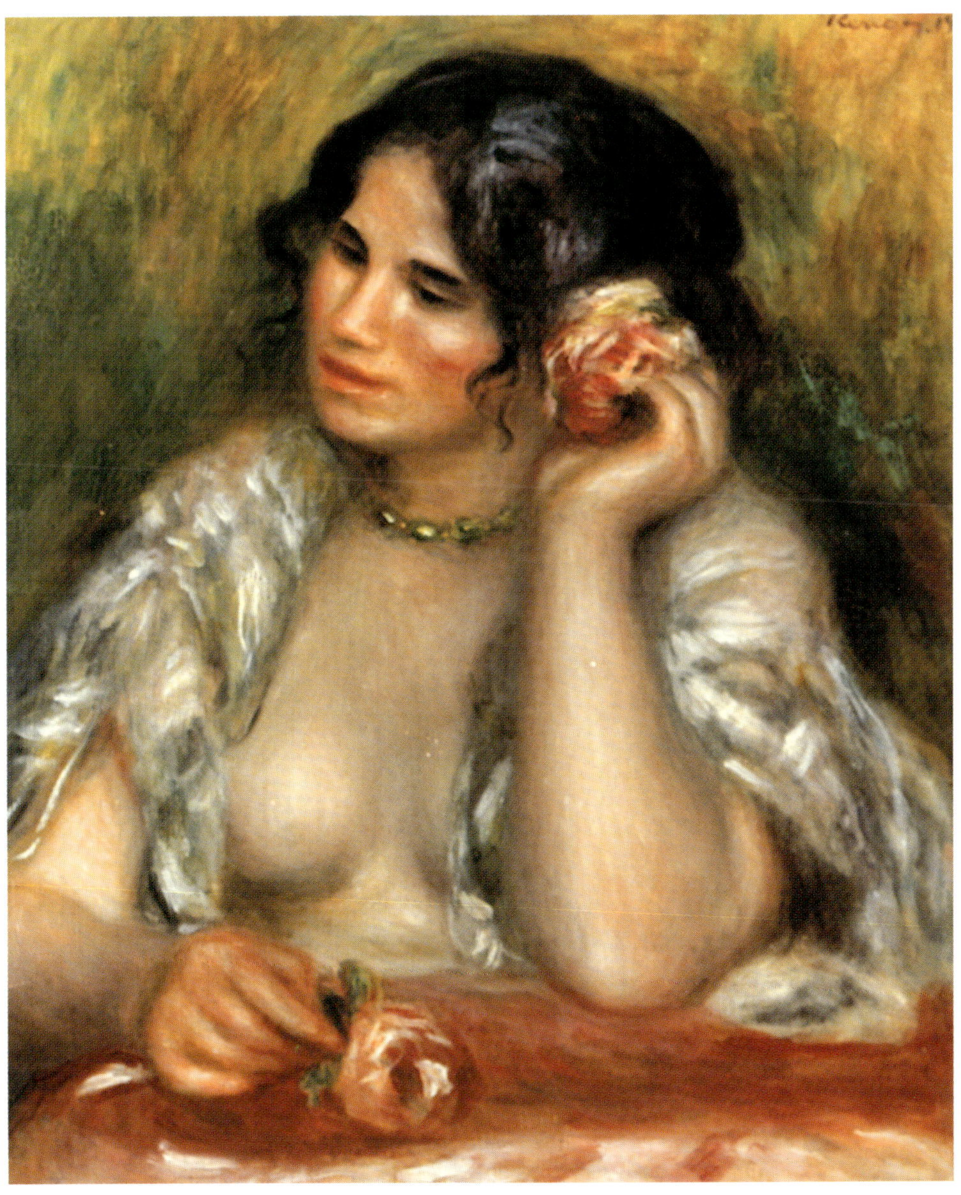

Gabrielle with a Rose, 1911 (Musée d'Orsay, Paris). This painting was the last in a series of paintings in which the nurse to Renoir's children, Gabrielle Renard, appears bare-breasted. At this point in his career Renoir was suffering from debilitating arthritis making the fluency with which this work was painted all the more remarkable. It is an example of his later work, in which his women have a richer, more mature aspect.

He wrote a great deal about his father in later years, in books that had a charm and allure equalled only by his father's own work.

Renoir explained his vision to his son, exposed the nature of his technique, which he never stopped developing. In 1918 he said, 'I'm trying to fuse the landscape with my figures; the old masters never attempted this.' He began to use paint less sparingly, creating thick, rich, sensual and textured strokes which became as much a part of the finished painting as the subject itself. He began to experiment with sculpture and when his arthritis made it impossible for him to work in that medium, he took on an assistant and borrowed a pair of hands. He designed a tapestry cartoon for the town of Lyons, and he returned to ceramics, with Coco, his youngest son.

His illness seems to have created in him a need for things physical. He could not feel things as he once had, and for a supremely tactile and sensual man, it was a travesty. He had always been obsessed by touch; he once told his son Jean, 'You must protect the ends of your fingers: if you expose them you may ruin your sense of touch and deprive yourself of a good deal of pleasure in life.'

His nudes became bigger, more robust, somehow warmer. He painted women at work in the fields, washing clothing, preparing for the bath. His strokes were broader, due to his illness, but his paintings retained their precision and eloquence. One of his most famous paintings of this time is *Washerwomen*, a rich celebration of a country woman's lot. He maintained the same ability to depict human interaction throughout his career; in the early years it manifested itself in his buoyant portrayals of Parisian café society, later he illustrated the relationship between his child and her nurse, or two maids in the garden. His latest works were in many ways his most honest, his most luminous. While Renoir did perhaps impart his own idealistic notions on to the subjects of his paintings, they smile believably and appear to savour the tasks at which they work. Renoir's world was an untroubled one; as a mature painter he was able to expand his gift for creating a world that was seamless and serene. His garden at Les Collettes became a haven, a place in which he could create a world unlike the one outside which had let him down.

Ambroise Vollard, a collector and dealer, and a good friend of the Renoir family, played an important role in Renoir's later life. With Renoir's approval he wrote a book about the painter, much maligned by the artist at the time, but clearly based on the versions of his story Renoir had resolved to tell him. Renoir painted Vollard in toreador garb in 1917, but earlier portraits of the dealer exist. It was Vollard who had encouraged Renoir's sculpture, when he found painting increasingly difficult, and he also arranged for Renoir to have a suitable assistant. Renoir wrote, 'When Vollard first mentioned sculpture, I told him to go to the devil, but on reflection I let myself be persuaded.'

Young Girls at the Piano, 1892 (Musée d'Orsay, Paris). One of four versions of this painting, which was purchased by the French state. Renoir was deeply unhappy with their choice, fretting that it was unpolished and unrepresentative of his work.

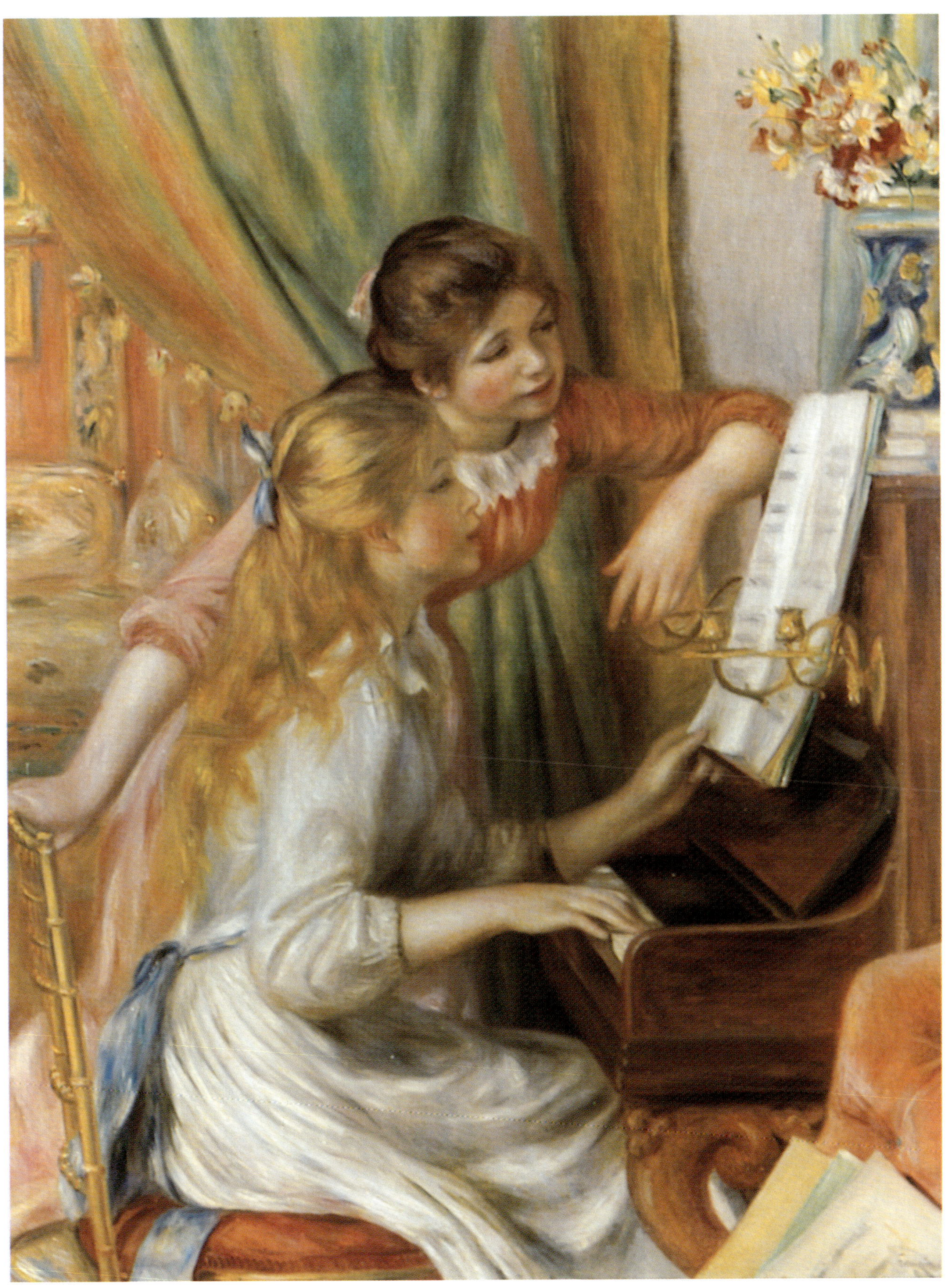

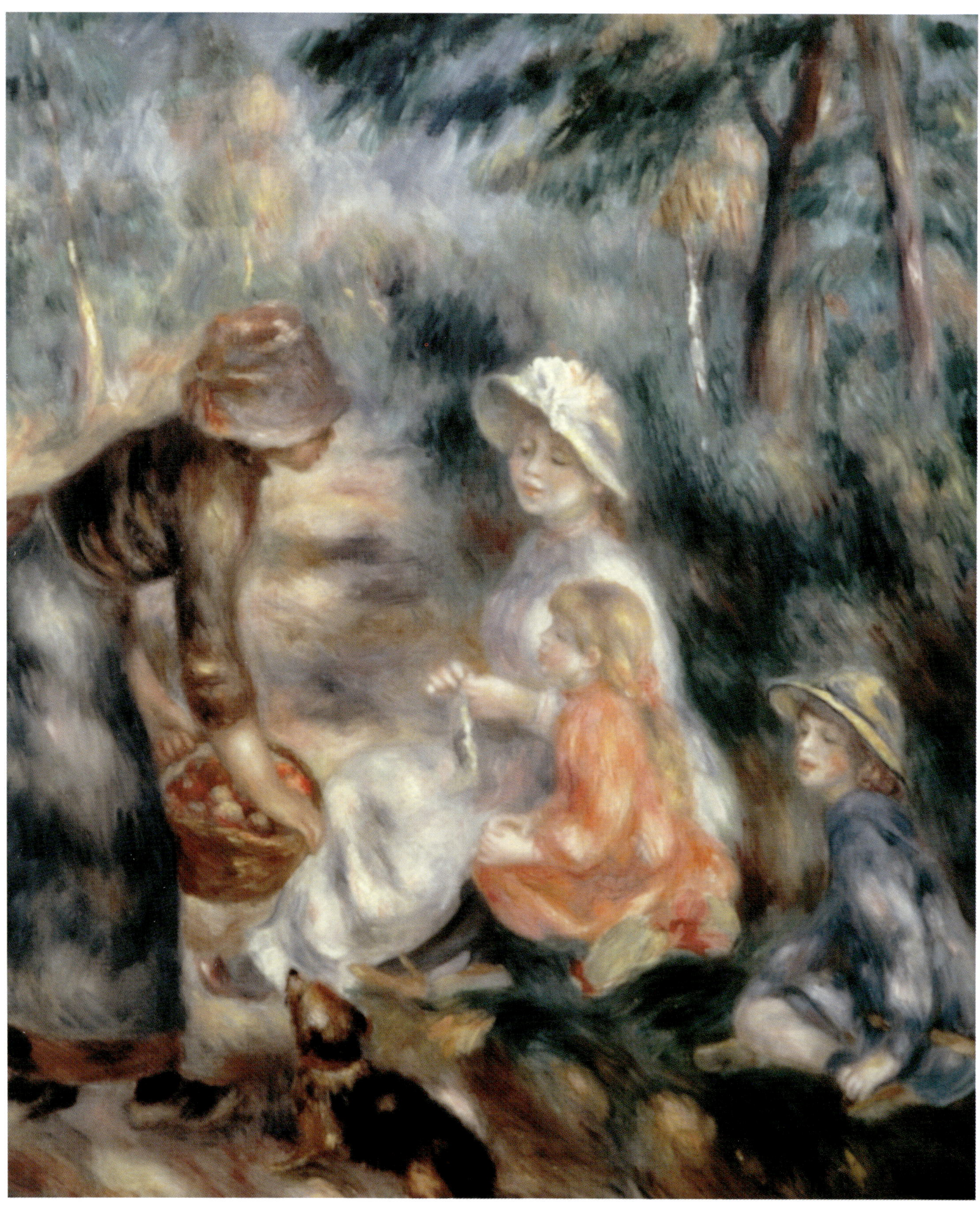

The early part of the twentieth century accorded him with the honours he truly deserved. He accepted, somewhat grudgingly, the award of Chevalier de la Legion d'Honneur in 1900, and in 1904 a major retrospective of his work took place at the Salon d'Automne, confirming his place as one of France's most important and influential painters.

With success, however, came the inevitable copies and, in the case of Renoir, a spate of absolute fakes. In 1903 Dr Georges Viau, a dentist, amateur painter and great Renoir collector was accused of having a number of forgeries of Renoir paintings and pastels. Renoir was shocked by the discovery and in January of 1904 he duly registered a complaint with the Procureur de la Republique, but following his lawyer's advice, he eventually withdrew it. Jean Renoir tells of his father repainting fakes which had been inadvertently purchased by his friends, rather than have their investment come to nothing.

Renoir continued to work until his death in 1919. When he could no longer hold a paintbrush, one was strapped to his hand, the skin protected by a handkerchief. His last great masterpiece, *The Bathers* (1918) is as rich and moving as any of his earlier work, his genius taking root in his mature years to become a tree of self-confidence, sensuality and above all unsurpassed joy. The painting is the supreme embodiment of his mature talents: splashes of paint applied with a sure and elegant touch; long languorous strokes caress the bodies of his bathers, whose faces seem to be flushed by arousal. Renoir created a stir of controversy with this work, but the gleeful energy with which it was evidently painted reveals perhaps that this was exactly the intention of the artist. The bather in the foreground was the beautiful model, Andrée Hessling, who later married Renoir's son Jean, the one behind appears to be an amalgamation of a number of Renoir's models, a woman created from the best qualities of each.

In order to paint with his now debilitating illness, the large canvas was placed on rollers on an adjustable easel. The painting in no way portrays the agony it must have caused the painter; his brushstrokes are as sure as ever, the light delicate upon the skin of his models whose flesh is almost tangible.

He had written in 1910 to the young painter Albert André, 'Happy painting, which, very late in life gives you illusions and sometimes joy' and he found a powerful sense of exultation in his work, about which, on the last day of his life, he was overheard to have said, 'I think I am beginning to understand something about it.'

When he died in Cagnes on 3 December 1919, the result of congestion of the lungs, a small still-life remained unfinished on his easel.

The Apple Seller, 1890 (Cleveland Museum of Art). The seated woman appears to be Renoir's wife Aline, and their son Pierre was likely the model for the boy on the right. The subject, like his *Washerwomen* series of paintings, presents an idyllic portrait of country life.

INDEX

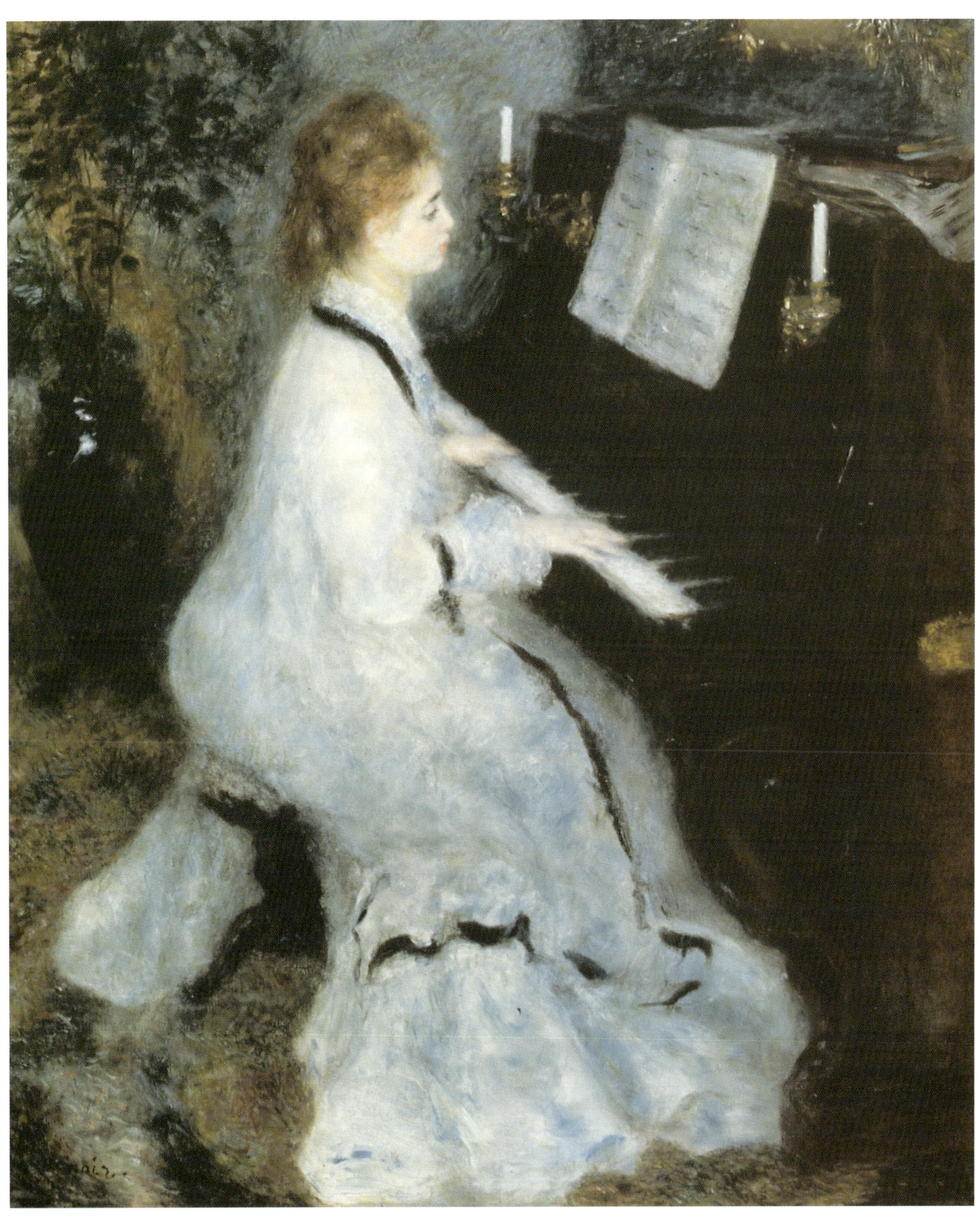

Renoir. Lady at the Piano, ***c.*** **1865**
(Chicago Institute of Art)

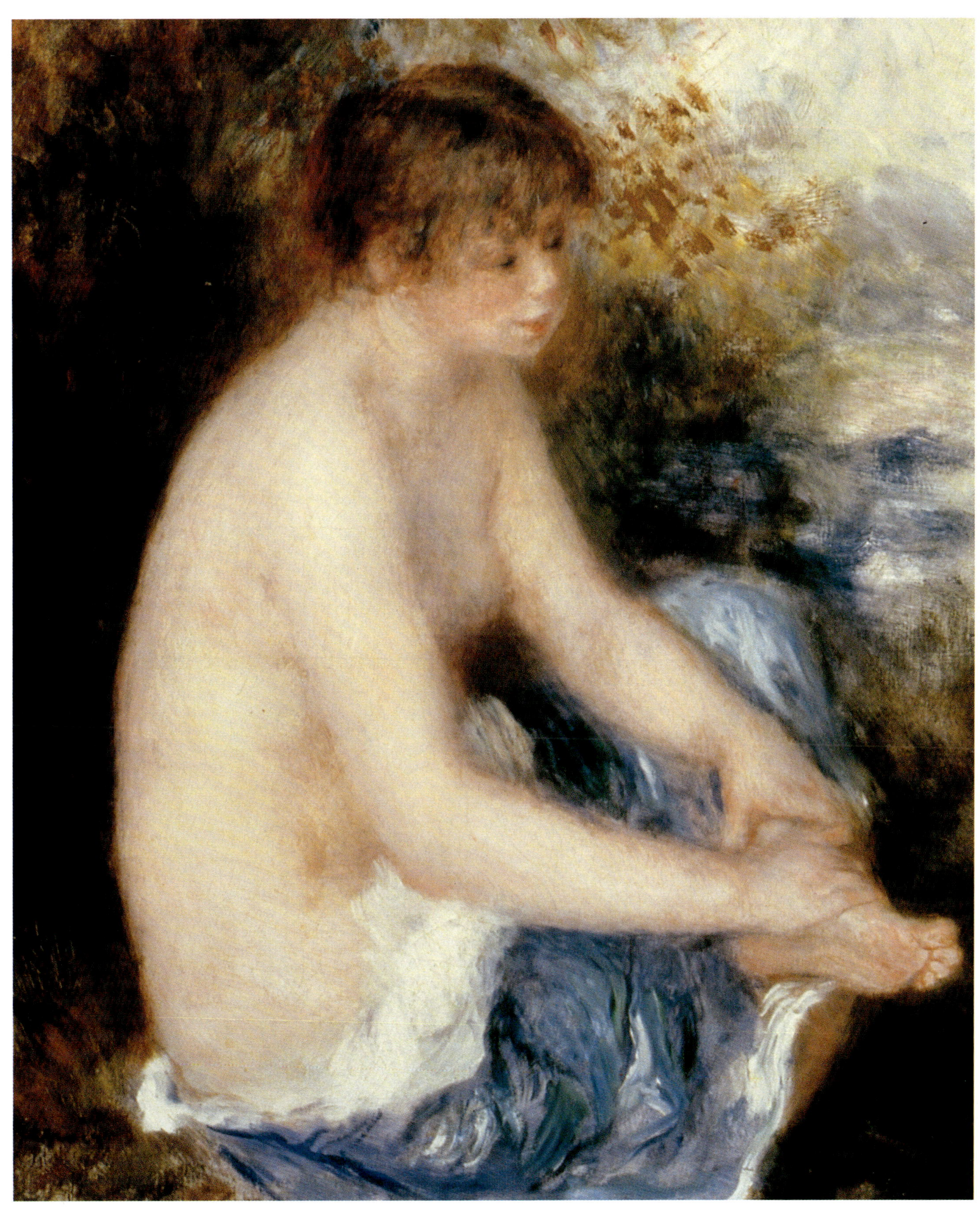

Renoir. Little Blue Nude, 1878
(Private collection)

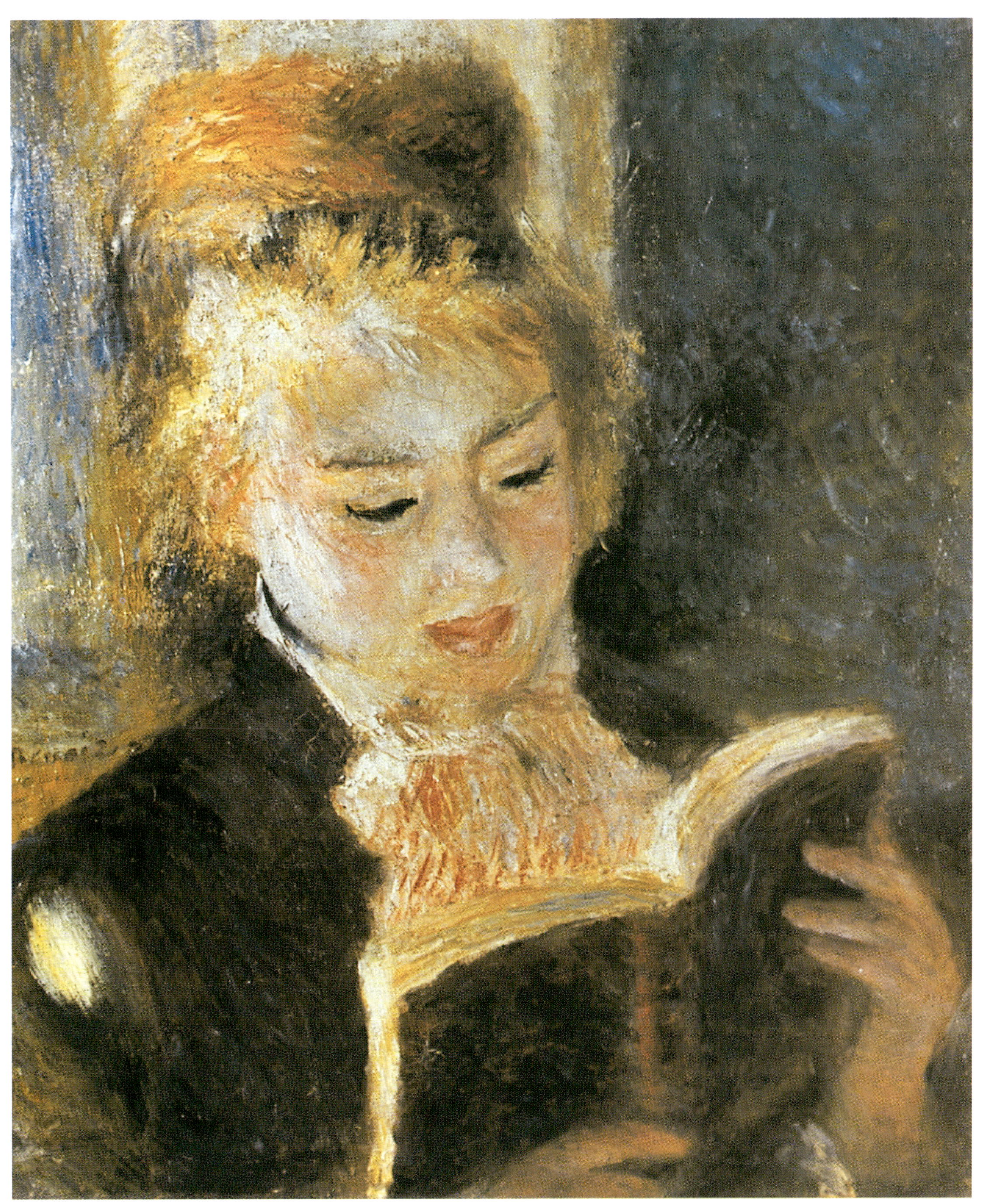

Renoir. Woman Reading, 1874
(Musée d'Orsay, Paris)

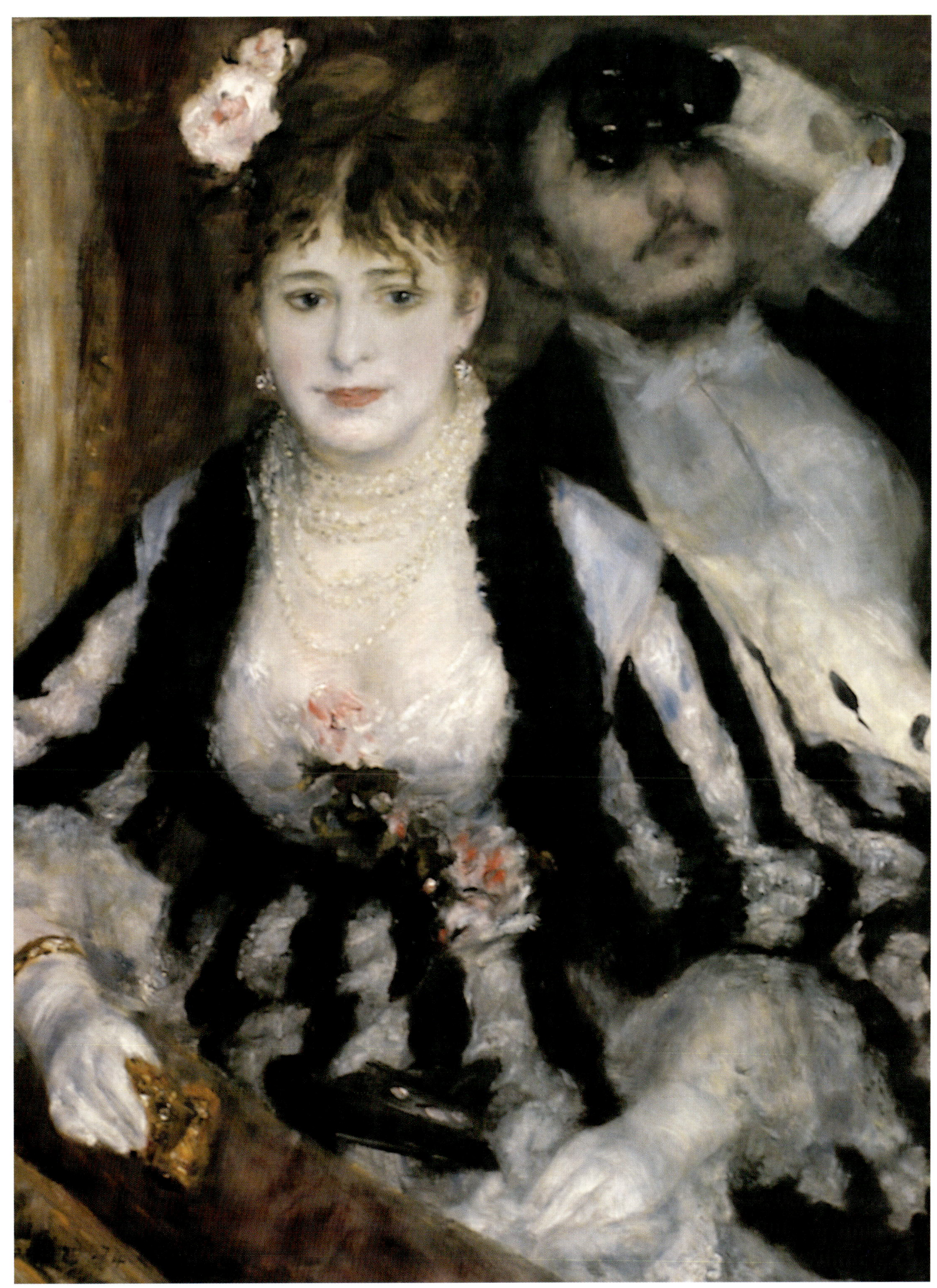

Renoir. La Loge, 1874
(Courthauld Institute, London)

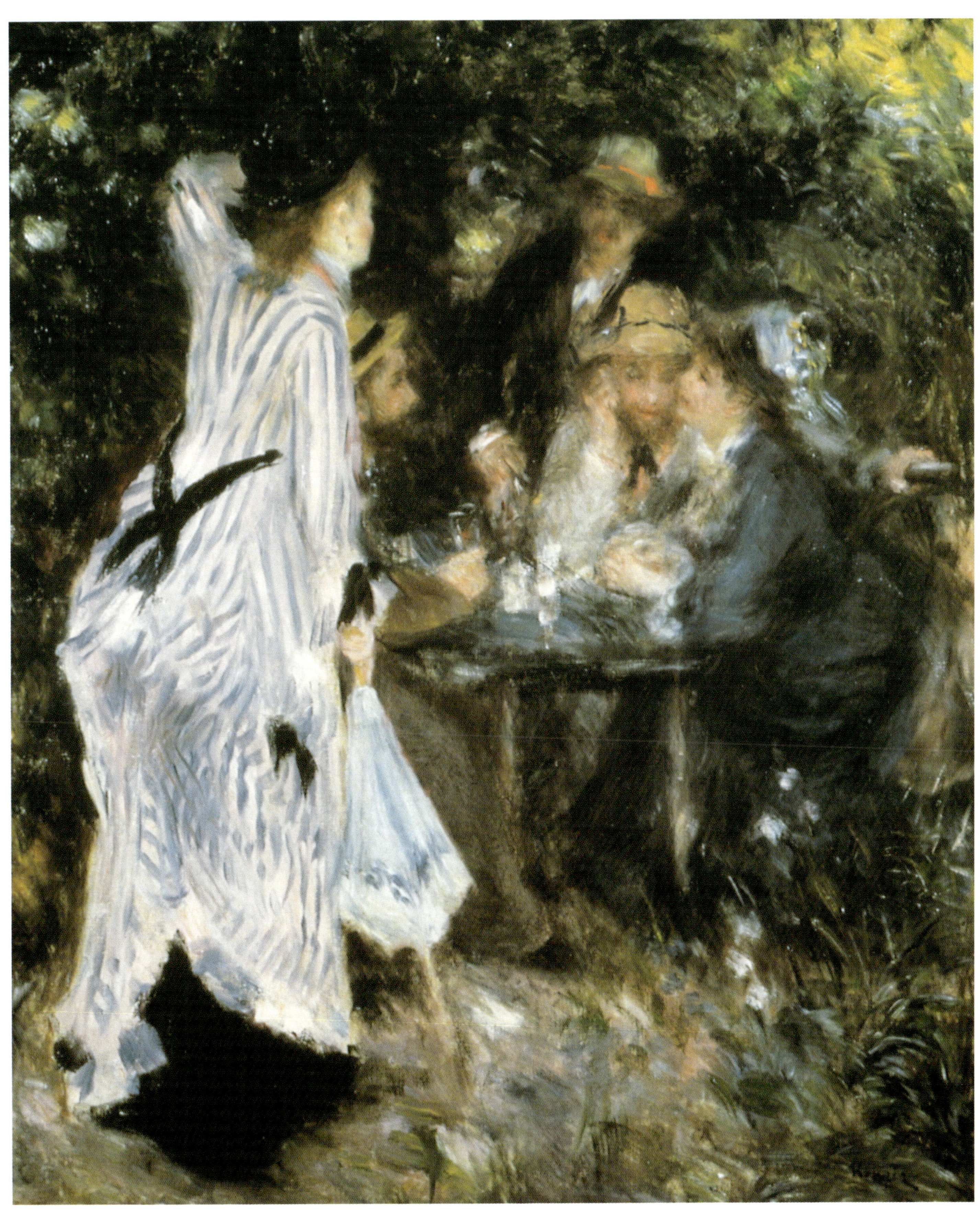

Renoir. Under the Arbour, Moulin de la Galette, 1876
(Pushkin Museum, Moscow)

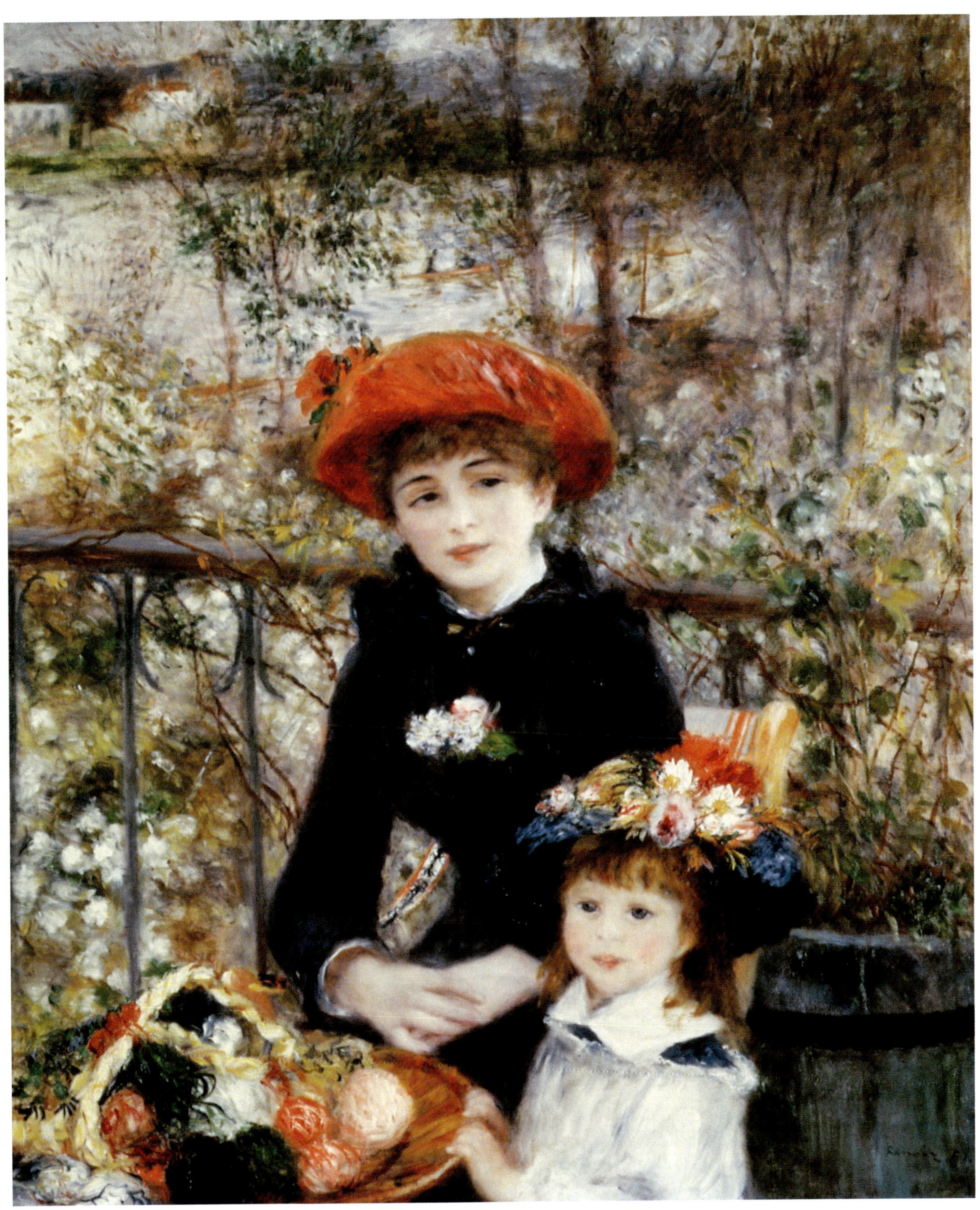

Renoir. On the Terrace, 1881
(Chicago Institute of Art)

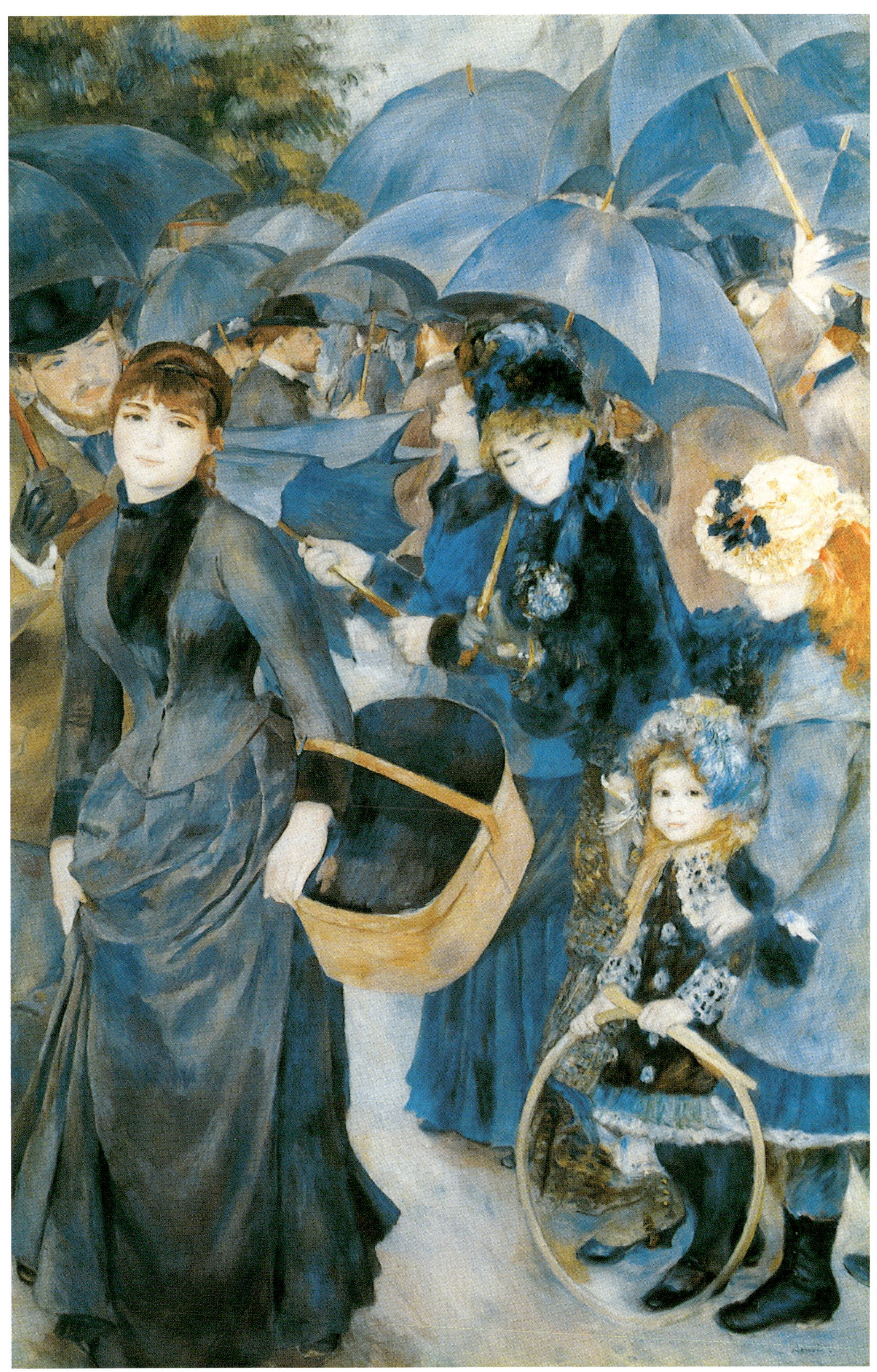

Renoir. The Umbrellas, 1881-5
(National Gallery, London)

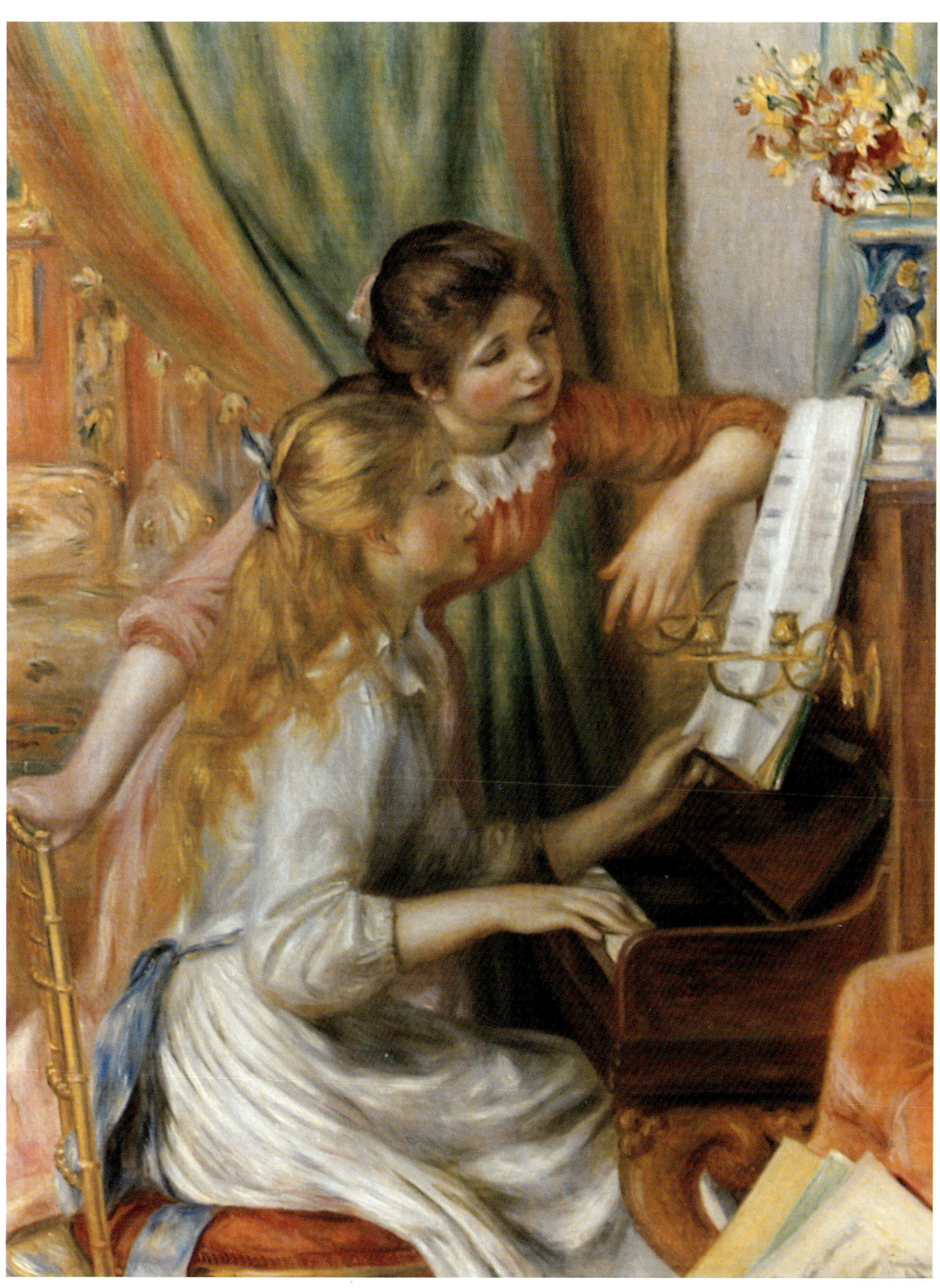

Renoir. Young Girls at the Piano, 1892
(Musée d'Orsay, Paris)